Annie's Favorite

Quick & Easy Projects™

Annie's Attic

Editorial Director
Andy Ashley

Production and Photography Director
Ange Van Arman

Design Manager
Marilyn Shelton

Design Staff
Mickie Akins, Sandy Kennebeck, Alice Vaughan,
Elizabeth Ann White

Senior Editor
Jennifer McClain

Project Editor
Donna Scott

Editorial Staff
Shirley Brown, Liz Field, Skeeter Gilson, Nina Marsh,
Shelly Riley

Photography Manager
Scott Campbell

Photography Staff
Tammy Coquat-Payne, Martha Coquat

Book Design & Production Manager
Diane Simpson

Color Specialist
Betty Holmes

Production Coordinator
Glenda Chamberlain

Library of Congress Cataloging-in-Publication Data
ISBN: 0-9655269-5-X
First Printing: 1999
Library of Congress Catalog Card Number: 99-73066
Published and Distributed by
Annie's Attic, LLC, Big Sandy, Texas 75755;
www.anniesattic.com
Printed in the United States of America

Table of Contents

Dear Crocheter

Do you ever feel like your day-to-day schedule is packed from morning till night? Do you wish you had more time to pursue your true love—crochet?

With the one-of-a-kind projects in this colorful and classic collection, it won't matter if you're racing across town to take your kitty for her check-up at the vet, only to be kept waiting! Playing taxi for the kids' piano or ballet lessons? Has the game gone into overtime at the high school gym? No problem!

Use those unused moments—in waiting rooms, ballgame half-times, when you're on the phone or even traveling—to create beautiful crochet projects!

Annie's Favorite Quick & Easy Projects™ is filled with almost 100 of my all-time fast-and-fun favorites, each and every one chosen to fit crochet into your busy day!

So don't let your hectic schedule get the best of you! Whether you're hurrying off to catch a plane or train, cheering at the baseball game or simply soaking up a few rays by the pool, the designs in Annie's Favorite Quick & Easy Projects™ will help you make the most of every moment!

Sincerely,

Annie

Special Days

When you're in need of just the right gift idea for that special occasion, look no further than the fast-and-fun projects in this chapter! From baby ideas to back to school bonanzas, they were chosen just for you!

Backpack

Designed by Dawn Kemp

Caution: Please use discretion when making items that have parts that could be swallowed, are sharp or are potentially harmful to small children.

Finished Size: 12" × 14" × 5¾".

Materials:
- ❏ Worsted yarn:
  - 15½ oz. off-white
  - 2½ oz. each green, blue, purple, orange, yellow and red
  - 1½ oz. each pink and gray
  - Small amount black
- ❏ 1½" round button
- ❏ Black fabric paint
- ❏ Tapestry needle
- ❏ F hook or hook needed to obtain gauge

Gauge: 9 sc = 2"; 9 sc rows = 2".

Basic Stitches: Ch, sl st, sc.

Notes: Each square on graph = 1 sc.

When **changing colors** *(see Stitch Guide)*, drop first color to wrong side of work, pick up when needed. Do not carry dropped color along back of work, use separate ball of yarn for each section of color and fasten off each color when no longer needed.

Front Side

Row 1: With off-white, ch 46, sc in second ch from hook, sc in each ch across, turn. *(45 sc made)*

Rows 2–58: Ch 1, sc in each st across, turn.

Rnd 59: Working around outer edge, ch 1, sc in each st and in end of each row around with 3 sc in each corner, join with sl st in first sc. Fasten off.

Rnd 60: Join blue with sc in any st, sc in each st around with 3 sc in each center corner st, join.

Rnd 61: Ch 1, sc in each st around with 3 sc in each center corner st, join. Fasten off.

Back Side

Rows 1–58: Repeat rows 1–58 of Front Side.

Rnd 59: Repeat rnd 59 of Front Side.

Rnds 60–61: With yellow, repeat rnds 60–61 of Front Side.

First End

Row 1: With off-white, ch 21, sc in second ch from hook, sc in each ch across, turn. *(20 sc made)*

Rows 2–3: Ch 1, sc in each st across, turn.

Row 4: Ch 1, sc in first 4 sts changing to gray *(see Stitch Guide)* in last st made, sc in next 4 sts changing to off-white in last st made, sc in next 4 sts changing to gray in last st made, sc in next 4 sts changing to off-white in last st made, sc in last 4 sts, turn.

Rows 5–58: Changing colors according to graphs on page 8, ch 1, sc in each st across, turn.

Rnd 59: Repeat rnd 59 of Front Side.

Rnds 60–61: With green, repeat rnds 60–61 of Front Side.

With black fabric paint, for screw, place dot at center of scissors.

Mark "1", "2" and "3" evenly spaced down ruler.

Second End

Row 1: With off-white, ch 21, sc in second ch from hook, sc in each ch across, turn. *(20 sc made)*

Row 2: Ch 1, sc in each st across, turn.

Rows 3–58: Changing colors according to graph on page 9, ch 1, sc in each st across, turn.

Rnd 59: Repeat rnd 59 of Front Side.

Rnds 60–61: With purple, repeat rnds 60–61 of Front Side.

With black fabric paint, mark pencil lead on pencil.

Bottom

Row 1: With off-white, ch 21, sc in second ch from hook, sc in each ch across, turn. *(20 sc made)*

Rows 2–45: Ch 1, sc in each st across, turn.

Rnd 46: Repeat rnd 59 of Front Side.

Rnds 47–48: With orange, repeat rnds 60–61 of Front Side.

Top

Row 1: With off-white, ch 46, sc in second ch from hook, sc in each ch across, turn. *(45 sc made)*

Rows 2: Ch 1, sc in each st across, turn.

Rows 3–28: Changing colors according to graph on page 9, ch 1, sc in each st across, turn.

Rnd 29: Repeat rnd 59 of Front Side.

Rnds 30–31: With red, repeat rnds 60–61 of Front Side.

With black fabric paint, write color name on each crayon. Write "My A-B-C and 1-2-3 Book" on book.

Buttonhole Flap

Row 1: Starting at bottom, with off-white, ch 13,

continued on page 8

Backpack

continued from page 7

sc in second ch from hook, sc in each ch across, turn. *(12 sc made)*

Row 2: Ch 1, sc in each st across, turn.

Row 3: Ch 1, sc in first 4 sts; for **buttonhole,** ch 4, skip next 4 sts; sc in last 4 sts, turn.

Row 4: Ch 1, sc in each stand in each ch across, turn.

Rows 5–12: Ch 1, sc in each st across, turn.

Rnd 13: Repeat rnd 59 of Front Side.

Rnds 14–15: With orange, repeat rnds 60–61 of Front Side.

Large Pocket

Row 1: With off-white, ch 16, sc in second ch from hook, sc in each ch across, turn. *(15 sc made)*

Row 2: Ch 1, sc in each st across, turn.

Rows 3–20: Changing colors according to graph on facing page, ch 1, sc in each st across, turn.

Rnd 21: Repeat rnd 59 of Front Side.

Rnds 22–23: With purple, repeat rnds 60–61 of Front Side.

With black fabric paint, write "Glue" centered on yellow section.

Small Pocket

Row 1: Starting at bottom, with off-white, ch 12, sc in second ch from hook, sc in each ch across, turn. *(11 sc made)*

Rows 3–10: Changing colors according to graph at right, ch 1, sc in each st across, turn.

Rnd 11: Repeat rnd 59 of Front Side.

Rnds 12–13: With green, repet rnds 60–61 of Front Side.

With black fabric paint, write "Eraser" centered on pink section.

Strap (make 2)

Row 1: With off-white, ch 7, sc in second ch from hook, sc in each ch across, turn. *(6 sc made)*

Rows 2–74: Or to desired length; ch 1, sc in each st across, turn.

Rnd 75: Repeat rnd 59 of Front Side.

Rnds 76–77: Repeat rnds 60–61 of Front Side.

Finishing

1: With right sides out, sew or sl st long ends of Sides and Ends together.

2: Sew or sl st Bottom to bottom edges of Sides and Ends.

3: Sew or sl st top edge of Top to top edge of Back Side.

4: Sew or sl st top edge of Buttonhole Flap centered to bottom edge of Top.

5: Sew sides and bottom of Large Pocket over rows 1–29 of Front Side 1" from left-hand edge. Sew sides and bottom of Small Pocket over rows 7–24 of Front Side 1" from right-hand edge.

6: Sew button centered to row 40 on Front Side.

7: Sew one end of one Strap ¾" from top and

other end ¾" from bottom on Back 1" from left-hand edge. Repeat with other Strap on right-hand side of Back. ♥

Small Pocket

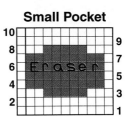

First End

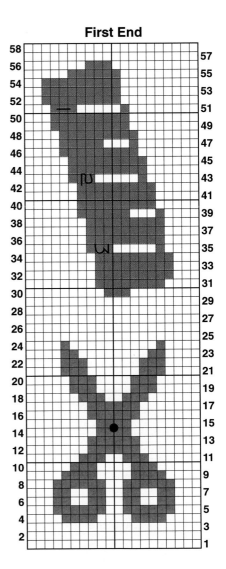

Top

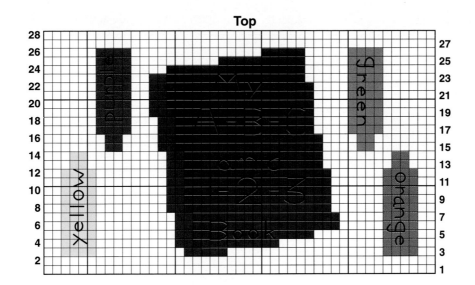

Large Pocket

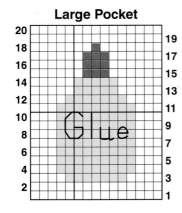

Second End

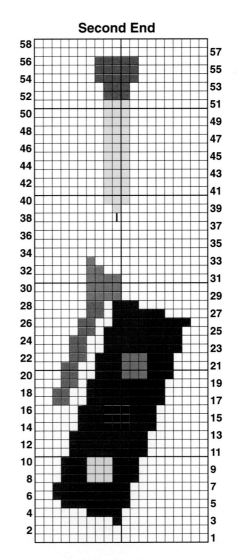

Colors

- ■ = Blue
- ■ = Orange
- ■ = Gray
- ☐ = Yellow
- ■ = Pink
- ■ = Purple
- ■ = Black
- ■ = Green
- ■ = Red
- ☐ = Off-White
- ⬛ = Black Fabric Paint

Easter Tree Ensemble

Designed by Mary Ann Colatuno

Finished Sizes: Pins and ornaments range in size from ¾" long to 2¾" long. Tree Skirt is 8½" across.

Materials:
- ❑ Size 10 crochet cotton thread:
  - 95 yds. variegated
  - 65 yds. pink
  - 55 yds. med. blue
  - 43 yds. white
  - 41 yds. yellow
  - 35 yds. lavender
  - 24 yds. ecru
  - 24 yds. silver metallic
  - 8 yds. orange
  - 4 yds. tan
  - 4 yds. green
  - 3 yds. lt. blue
- ❑ ⅛"-wide ribbon:
  - 2 yds. white
  - 10" med. pink
  - 7" ecru
- ❑ ¼"-wide ribbon:
  - 12" purple
  - 10" lt. blue
  - 10" pink
  - 6" dk. blue
  - 6" silver
- ❑ Small ribbon roses:
  - 2 lt. blue
  - 1 each silver, lt. pink, med. pink and white
- ❑ Miniature decorative eggs:
  - 2 plastic eggs
  - 2 wooden eggs
- ❑ 6" of white and 8" of ecru 3mm strung beads
- ❑ 4 pair of 3mm wiggle eyes
- ❑ 2 pink ⅛" pom-poms
- ❑ White ¼" pom-pom
- ❑ Small amount Spanish moss and baby's breath flowers
- ❑ 2 pin backs
- ❑ Polyester fiberfill
- ❑ Aluminum foil
- ❑ Plastic wrap
- ❑ Fabric stiffener
- ❑ Craft glue
- ❑ Nos. 7 and 10 steel hooks

Basic Stitches: Ch, sl st, sc, hdc, dc.

Notes: Use No. 10 hook on all items except Tree Skirt.

Work in continuous rnds; do not join or turn unless otherwise stated. Mark first st of each rnd.

When **changing colors** *(see Stitch Guide),* always change color in last st made and fasten off color not being used.

continued on page 12

Easter Tree Ensemble

continued from page 11

Bunny Angel

Rnd 1: Starting at top of Head, with white, ch 2, 6 sc in second ch from hook. *(6 sc made)*

Rnd 2: 2 sc in each st around. *(12)*

Rnds 3–4: Sc in each st around.

Rnd 5: (Sc in next st, skip next st) around. *(6)*

Rnd 6: For **Neck,** 2 sc in each st around. *(12)* Stuff.

Rnd 7: (Sc in next st, 2 sc in next st) around, changing to pink in last st made *(see Notes).* *(18)*

Rnd 8: For **Dress,** (sc in each of next 2 sts, 2 sc in next st) around. *(24)*

Rnd 9: 2 sc in each st around. *(48)*

Rnd 10: Sc in first 12 sts; for **armhole,** skip next 12 sts; sc in next 12 sts; for **armhole,** skip last 12 sts, join with sl st in first sc. *(24)*

Rnd 11: Ch 1, sc in each st around, join.

Rnd 12: (Ch 3, sc) in first st, skip next st; for **sc-V st,** *(sc, ch 2, sc) in next st, skip next st; repeat from * around, join with sl st in first ch of ch-3. *(12 sc V sts)*

Rnd 13: Ch 1, sc-V st in first ch sp, sc in next sp between sc-V sts, (sc-V st in next ch sp, sc in next sp between sc-V sts) around, join with sl st in first sc. *(12 sc-V sts, 12 sc)*

Rnds 14–16: Ch 1, sc-V st in first ch sp, sc in next sc between sc-V sts, (sc-V st in next ch sp, sc in next sc between sc-V sts) around, join.

Rnd 17: Ch 1, sc in first ch sp; for **picot, ch 3, sl st in third ch from hook;** sc in next sc between sc-V sts, picot, (sc in next ch sp, picot, sc in next sc between sc-V sts, picot) around, join. Fasten off.

Sleeves

Working in skipped sts of rnd 9 on one armhole, join pink with sl st in first st, (picot, sc in next st) 10 times, picot, skip next st, join with sl st in first sc. Fasten off.

Repeat Sleeve on other armhole.

Ear (make 2)

With white, ch 5, sc in second ch from hook, sc in each of next 2 chs, 3 sc in last ch *(this is top of Ear);* working on opposite side of ch, sc in each of next 3 chs, join with sl st in first sc. Fasten off.

Bunny Pin

Rnds 1–6: Work rnds 1–6 of Bunny Angel.

Rnd 7: (Sc in next st, 2 sc in next st) around, changing to variegated in last st made. *(18)*

Rnds 8–17: Work rnds 8–17 of Bunny Angel.

Sleeves

Using variegated, work same as Bunny Angel Sleeves.

Ear (make 2)

Work same as Bunny Angel Ear.

Chicken Angel

Rnds 1–6: Using yellow, work rnds 1–6 of Bunny Angel.

Rnd 7: (Sc in next st, 2 sc in next st) around, changing to med. blue in last st made. *(18)*

Rnds 8–17: Work rnds 8–17 of Bunny Angel.

Sleeves

Using med. blue, work same as Bunny Angel Sleeves.

Beak

Row 1: With orange, ch 2, sc in second ch from hook, turn. *(1 sc made)*

Row 2: Ch 1, 2 sc in next st, turn. *(2)*

Row 3: Ch 1, sc in each st across, turn.

Row 4: Ch 1, sc next 2 sts tog. Fasten off. *(1)*

Tail

With yellow, ch 6, dc in third ch from hook, hdc in next ch, sc in next ch, sl st in last ch; working in remaining lps on opposite side of ch, sc in each of next 3 chs, join with sl st in top of ch 3. Fasten off. Tack to center back of Dress over rnd 15.

Chicken Pin

Rnds 1–6: Using yellow, work rnds 1–6 of Bunny Angel.

Rnd 7: (Sc in next st, 2 sc in next st) around, changing to variegated in last st made. *(18)*

Rnds 8–17: Work rnds 8–17 of Bunny Angel.

Sleeves

Using variegated, work same as Bunny Angel Sleeves.

Beak

Work same as Chicken Angel Beak.

Tail

Work same as Chicken Angel Tail.

Silver Angel

Rnds 1–6: Using tan, work rnds 1–6 of Bunny Angel.

Rnd 7: (Sc in next st, 2 sc in next st) around changing to metallic in last st made. *(18)*

Rnds 8–17: Work rnds 8–17 of Bunny Angel.

Sleeves

Using metallic, work same as Bunny Angel Sleeves.

Ecru Angel

Rnds 1–6: Using ecru, work rnds 1–6 of Bunny Angel.

Rnd 7: (Sc in next st, 2 sc in next st) around. *(18)*

Rnds 8–17: Work rnds 8–17 of Bunny Angel.

Sleeves

Using ecru, work same as Bunny Angel Sleeves.

Pink Hat

Rnd 1: With pink, ch 2, 6 sc in second ch from hook. *(6 sc made)*

Rnd 2: 2 sc in each st around. *(12)*

Rnds 3–5: Sc in each st around.

Rnd 6: Working this rnd in **back lps** *(see Stitch Guide)*, 2 sc in each st around, join with sl st in first sc. *(24)*

Rnd 7: (Ch 3, hdc) in first st, skip next st; for **hdc-V st, *(hdc, ch 2, hdc)** in next st, skip next st; repeat from * around, join with sl st in second ch of ch-3. *(12 hdc-V sts)*

Rnd 8: Ch 1, (sc, picot, sc) in first ch sp, sc in next sp between hdc-V sts, *(sc, picot, sc) in next ch sp, picot, sc in next sp between hdc-V sts; repeat from * around, join with sl st in first sc. Fasten off.

Variegated Hat (make 2)

Rnds 1–7: With variegated, repeat rnds 1–7 of Pink Hat.

Rnd 8: Ch 1, sc in first ch sp, picot, sc in next sp between hdc-V sts, picot, (sc in next ch sp, picot, sc in next sp between hdc-V sts, picot) around, join with sl st in first sc. Fasten off.

Carrot

Row 1: Starting at bottom, with orange, ch 2, 2 sc in second ch from hook, turn. *(2 sc made)*

Row 2: Ch 1, 2 sc in first st, sc in next st, turn. *(3)*

Row 3: Ch 1, 2 sc in first st, sc in each of last 2 sts, turn. *(4)*

Row 4: Ch 1, 2 sc in first st, sc in each of next 2 sts, 2 sc in last st, turn. *(6)*

Row 5: Ch 1, sc in each st across, turn.

Row 6: Ch 1, 2 sc in first st, sc in next 4 sts, 2 sc in last st, turn. *(8)*

Rows 7–8: Ch 1, sc in each st across, turn.

Row 9: Ch 1, sc in each st across changing to green in last made, turn.

Row 10: Ch 1, sc in each st across, turn.

Row 11: For **leaves**, ch 1, (sc, ch 12, sc) in each st across. Fasten off.

Fold Carrot in half lengthwise, matching ends of rows; working through both thicknesses, join orange with sl st in end of row 1, sl st in next 9 rows. Fasten off. Stuff lightly. Sew top opening closed.

Cut 10" piece from ribbon for hanger. Fold ribbon in half; glue ends to center top of Carrot.

Egg

Rnd 1: With lt. blue, ch 2, 4 sc in second ch from hook. *(4 sc made)*

Rnd 2: 2 sc in each st around. *(8)*

Rnd 3: (Sc in next st, 2 sc in next st) around. *(12)*

Rnd 4: Sc in each st around.

Rnd 5: (Sc in next st, sc next 2 sts tog) around. *(8)* Stuff.

Rnds 6–7: (Sc next 2 sts tog) around. *(4, 2)*

Rnd 8: Sl st next 2 sts tog, join with sl st in first sl st. Fasten off.

Cut 6" piece and 4" piece from white ⅛" ribbon. Glue ends of 4" ribbon to center top of Egg for hanger. Tie 6" piece in a tiny bow. Trim ends. Glue bow to center top of Egg over hanger ends; glue one blue ribbon rose to center of bow.

Tree Skirt

Row 1: With No. 7 hook and variegated, ch 25, 2 dc in fourth ch from hook, 2 dc in each ch across changing to lavender in last st made, turn. *(45 dc made)*

Row 2: Ch 3, (2 dc in next st, dc in next st) across changing to yellow in last st made, turn. *(67)*

Row 3: Ch 3, dc in next st, (2 dc in next st, dc in each of next 2 sts) 21 times, 2 dc in next st, dc in last st changing to med. blue, turn. *(89)*

Row 4: Ch 3, dc in each of next 2 sts, 2 dc in next st, (dc in each of next 3 sts, 2 dc in next st) 21 times, dc in last st changing to pink, turn. *(111)*

Row 5: Ch 3, dc in each st across changing to white in last st made, turn.

Row 6: Ch 3, dc in each st across changing to variegated in last made, turn.

Row 7: (Ch 4, dc) in first st, *ch 1, skip next st; for **dc-V st, (dc, ch 1, dc)** in next st; repeat from * across changing to lavender in last st made, turn. *(56 dc-V sts)*

Row 8: (Sl st, ch 3, dc, ch 1, 2 dc) in first ch sp, (2 dc, ch 1, 2 dc) in ch sp of each dc-V st across changing to yellow in last st made, turn.

Row 9: Sl st in each of first 2 sts, (sl st, ch 3, dc, ch 1, 2 dc) in first ch sp, (2 dc, ch 1, 2 dc) in each ch sp across changing to med. blue in last st made, turn.

Row 10: Sl st in each of first 2 sts, (sl st, ch 3, dc, ch 1, 2 dc) in first ch sp, (2 dc, ch 1, 2 dc) in each ch sp across changing to pink in last st made, turn.

Row 11: Sl st in each of first 2 sts, (sl st, ch 3, dc, ch 2, 2 dc) in first ch sp, (2 dc, ch 2, 2 dc) in each ch sp across changing to white in last st made, turn.

Rnd 12: Working around entire outer edge, sl st in each of first 2 sts, (sl st, ch 3, dc, sl st, ch 3, dc, sl st) in first ch sp, (2 dc, sl st, ch 3, dc, sl st) in each ch sp across; working in ends of rows and in opposite side of starting ch on row 1, 2 sc in end of each row and sc in each ch across, join with sl st in first sl st. Fasten off.

Cut 20" piece from white ⅛" ribbon. Weave ribbon through sts on row 1 of Skirt.

Finishing

1: Using a crochet Dress as pattern, shape aluminum foil into two cones.

2: Apply stiffener to Bunny and Chicken Angels, Bunny and Chicken Pins, Bunny Ears and Hats according to manufacturer's instructions.

continued on page 15

Apple Pencil Holder

Designed by Florence O'Connor

Finished Size: 3¼" tall.

Materials:
- ❏ Worsted yarn:
  - 2 oz. red
  - Small amount each green and yellow
- ❏ 4½ oz. baby food jar
- ❏ Two 3mm wiggly eyes
- ❏ Craft glue
- ❏ Polyester fiberfill
- ❏ Tapestry needle
- ❏ E hook or hook needed to obtain gauge

Gauge: 5 sc = 1"; 5 sc rows = 1".

Basic Stitches: Ch, sl st, sc, hdc, dc.

Note: Work in continuous rnds; do not join or turn unless otherwise stated. Mark first st of each rnd.

Apple

Rnd 1: Starting at bottom, with red, ch 2, 8 sc in second ch from hook. *(8 sc made)*

Rnd 2: (2 sc in next st, sc in next st) around. *(12)*

Rnd 3: 2 sc in each st around. *(24)*

Rnd 4: (Sc in next 5 sts, 2 sc in next st) around. *(28)*

Rnd 5: (Sc in next 5 sts, 2 sc in each of next 2 sts) around. *(36)*

Rnd 6: (Sc in next 5 sts, sc in next 4 sts) around.

Rnd 7: (Sc in next st, 2 sc in next st) around. *(54 sc)*

Rnds 8–9: Sc in each st around.

Rnd 10: Sc in each of first 2 sts, sc next 2 sts tog, (sc in next 11 sts, sc next 2 sts tog), sc in next 12 sts, sc next 2 sts tog; repeat between ( ), sc in last 10 sts. *(50)*

Rnd 11: Sc in each of first 2 sts, sc next 2 sts tog, sc in next 11 sts, sc next 2 sts tog, (sc in next 10 sts, sc next 2 sts tog) 2 times, sc in last 9 sts. *(46)*

Rnd 12: Sc in first st, (sc next 2

sts tog) 2 times, sc in next 8 sts, *(sc next 2 sts tog) 2 times, sc in next 7 sts; repeat from * 2 more times. *(38)*

Rnds 13–14: Sc in each st around.

Rnd 15: Sc in each of first 2 sts, (2 sc in next st, sc in each of next 3 sts) around. *(47)*

Rnd 16: Sc in each st around.

Rnd 17: (Sc in next 6 sts, 2 sc in next st) 6 times, sc in last 5 sts. *(53)*

Rnds 18–19: Sc in each st around.

Rnd 20: Sc in each of first 2 sts, (sc next 2 sts tog, sc in next st) around. *(36)*

Insert jar. Stuff around jar. Continue stuffing as you work.

Rnd 21: (Sc in next st, sc next 2 sts tog) around. *(24)*

Rnd 22: Sc in each st around.

Rnd 23: (Sc in next st, sc next 2 sts tog) around. *(16)*

Rnd 24: Sl st in each st around, join with sl st in first sl st. Fasten off.

Leaf (make 2)

With green, ch 8, sl st in second ch from hook, sc in next ch, hdc in next ch, dc in each of next 2 chs, hdc in next ch, 2 sc in last ch; working in remaining lps on opposite side of starting ch, hdc in next ch, dc in each of next 2 chs, hdc in next ch, sc in next ch, sl st in last ch, join with sl st in first sl st. Fasten off.

Tack bottom of Leaves overlapped on top of Apple.

Worm

Rnd 1: With yellow, ch 4, sl st in first ch to form ring, ch 1, sc in each ch around. *(4 sc made)*

Rnds 2–10: Sc in each st around. At end of last rnd, join with sl st in first sc. Leaving 8" for sewing, fasten off. Sew rnd 10 closed.

Glue eyes to rnd 9 of Worm ¼" apart.

Sew rnd 1 of Worm to rnds 19 and 20 of Apple opposite Leaves. ♥

Easter Tree Ensemble

continued from page 13

3: Place dampened Bunny and Chicken Angel on foil cones, shaping Sleeves and Dresses as they dry. Remove from foil cones. Cover flat surface with plastic wrap. Place dampened Ears on flat surface. Stuff small amount of plastic wrap inside each Hat, shape and place on surface. Stuff a small amount of plastic wrap inside Bunny Pin and Chicken Pin; flatten and place on surface. Remove all items from plastic wrap when completely dry.

4: Glue one pair of eyes to front of each Bunny and Chicken Head over rnds 2 and 3.

5: Glue each pair of Bunny Ears to back of each Bunny Head.

6: Glue one pink pom-pom to each Bunny Head directly below eyes for nose. Glue white pom-pom to center back of rnd 12 on Bunny Angel for tail.

7: Fold each Chicken Beak in half, glue the folds to each Chicken Head between rnds 3 and 4 below eyes.

8: For each Angel and Pin, tie a 6" matching or coordinating color ribbon in small bow and glue to front of Dress *(see photo)*. Glue matching or coordinating ribbon rose, beaded trim or miniature egg to center of bow.

9: For each Bunny and Chicken Pin, glue variegated Hat to back of Head; glue pin back to center back of Dress and brim on Hat.

10: For Silver and Ecru Angels, glue small amount Spanish moss to Head for hair. Cut a 3" piece from silver metallic thread and strung beads, shape each into a halo and glue to top of Angel's Head *(see photo)*. Glue a sprig of baby's breath in Silver Angel's hair.

11: Tie an 8" piece white ribbon in a bow around crown on Pink Hat. Trim ends of ribbon to desired length. Glue white strung beads to bow. Glue three desired color ribbon roses over middle of bow. For hanging loop, cut two pieces each 2½" long from white ribbon. Tie one end of each 2½" piece together; glue other ends to back of Hat.

12: For each hanging loop except Pink Hat, cut a matching or coordinating piece of ribbon or thread in desired length, tie ends together in a knot. Glue knot to back of ornament so it hangs evenly. ♥

Basket Full of Love

Designed by Beth Mueller

Finished Size: About 12" × 20½".

Materials:
- ❑ 7 oz. each white and rose worsted yarn
- ❑ Two 12" × 20½" pieces muslin fabric
- ❑ Polyester fiberfill
- ❑ White sewing thread
- ❑ Sewing needle
- ❑ G crochet hook or hook needed to obtain gauge

Gauge: 4 sc = 1"; 4 sc rows = 1".

Basic Stitches: Ch, sl st, sc.

Note: When **changing colors** *(see Stitch Guide),* drop first color to wrong side of work, pick up again when needed. Always change colors in last st made. Carry dropped yarn along wrong side of work and cover dropped yarn with stitches as you work.

Side A
Row 1: With white, ch 82, sc in second ch from hook, sc in each ch across, turn. *(81 sc made) Back of row 1 is right side of work.*

Rows 2–45: Ch 1; changing colors according to corresponding row on graph on page -, sc in each st across, turn.

Row 46: Ch 1, sc in each st across. Fasten off.

Side B
Rows 1–46: Reversing colors, repeat rows 1–46 of Side A.

Pillow Form
With sewing needle and white thread, allowing ¼" for seams, sew the two muslin pieces right sides together leaving an opening for turning and stuffing. Turn right side out, stuff and sew opening closed.

Edging
Holding the two crocheted pieces wrong sides together and working through both Sides, join white with sc in end of row 1 at bottom right corner, (ch 3, skip next row, sc in next row) 22 times, (ch 3, sc in corner) 3 times, (ch 3, skip next st, sc in next st) 39 times, (ch 3, sc in corner) 3 times, (ch 3, skip next row, sc in next row) 22 times, (ch 3, sc in corner) 3 times; insert Pillow Form, (ch 3, skip next ch, sc in next ch) 39 times, (ch 3, sc in corner) 2 times, ch 3, join with sl st in first sc. Fasten off. ♥

Wedding Album Cover

Designed by Maria Nagy

Finished Size: Approximately 11" × 10" × 2¼".

Materials:
- ❑ 9½ oz. white worsted yarn
- ❑ 2 yds. white 1¼"-wide lace ribbon
- ❑ 2 yds. white 3⁄16"-wide satin ribbon
- ❑ 5"-diameter metal ring
- ❑ Silk bridal flower spray
- ❑ 2 white 8" × 12" fabric pieces
- ❑ 10"-wide × 11½"-high × 2¾"-thick photo album
- ❑ White sewing thread
- ❑ Tapestry and sewing needles
- ❑ F hook or hook needed to obtain gauge

Gauge: 9 dc = 2"; 4 dc and 4 sc rows = 3".

Basic Stitches: Ch, sl st, sc, dc.

Cover
Row 1: Beginning at front, ch 41, sc in second ch from hook, sc in each ch across, turn. *(40 sc made)*

Row 2: Ch 3 *(counts as dc)*, dc in each st across, turn. *Front of row 2 is right side of work.*

Row 3: Ch 1, sc in each st across, turn.

Rows 4–67: Repeat rows 2 and 3 alternately.

Rnd 68: For **edging,** working around outer edge, ch 1, sc in first st, *(ch 4, skip next 2 sts, sc in next st) 13 times; working in ends of rows, ch 4, sc in end of first row, (ch 4, skip next dc row, sc in end of next sc row) 33 times, ch 4*; working on opposite side of starting ch on row 1, sc in first ch; repeat between first and second *, join with sl st in first sc.

Rnds 69–70: Ch 1, sc in first ch sp, ch 5, (sc in next ch sp, ch 5) around, join. At end of last rnd, fasten off.

Picture Frame
Rnd 1: Working around ring *(see Stitch Guide),* join with sl st around ring, ch 3, work 89 dc around ring, join with sl st in top of ch-3. *(90 dc made)*

Rnd 2: Ch 1, sc in first st, ch 3, skip next st, (sc in next st, ch 3, skip next st) around, join with sl st in first sc.

Rnds 3–4: Ch 1, sc in first ch sp, ch 4, (sc in next ch sp, ch 4) around, join. At end of last rnd, fasten off.

Finishing
1: For **pockets,** fold one long edge of each fabric piece under ⅛", fold under again ¼" and hem. Press all other edges under ⅛".

2: Matching unhemmed long edges to row 1 and row 66, sew three unhemmed edges of each fabric piece to inside of Cover leaving hemmed edges unsewn.

3: Make a 5"-wide multi-loop bow from lace ribbon. Tie 24" of 3⁄16" ribbon around center of lace bow. Weave remaining ribbon through sts on rnd 1 of Picture Frame, tie ends in bow around lace bow.

4: Center and sew Picture Frame to front of Cover at top. Sew bridal flower spray to Cover below bottom of Picture Frame.

5: Insert front and back photo album cover into fabric pocket. ♥

Fisherman's Basket

Designed by Ann Ferguson

Finished Size: 7½" tall.

Materials:
- ❑ 100 yds. 3-ply jute twine or two of strands rug yarn held together
- ❑ Small amount brown worsted yarn
- ❑ 4 brown sheets 7-mesh plastic canvas
- ❑ Fishing fly with leader
- ❑ Fish-shaped lure
- ❑ Sewing thread to match jute
- ❑ Sewing and tapestry needles
- ❑ M/13 wooden hook or hook needed to obtain gauge

Gauge: 2 sc = 1"; 2 sc rows = 1".

Basic Stitches: Ch, sl st, sc.

Note: Use jute unless otherwise stated. Remove hooks from fly and lure.

Bottom
Row 1: Ch 21, sc in second ch from hook, sc in each ch across, turn. *(20 sc made)*
Rows 2–3: Ch 1, sc in each st across, turn.
Rows 4–5: Ch 1, sc first 2 sts tog, sc in each st across to last 2 sts, sc last 2 sts tog, turn. At end of last row *(16)*.
Rows 6–8: Ch 1, sc in each st across, turn.
Rows 9–12: Ch 1, sc first 2 sts tog, sc in each st across to last 2 sts, sc last 2 sts tog, turn. At end of last row, fasten off. *(8)*
Using Bottom as pattern, cut two pieces from plastic canvas ⅛" smaller on all edges for lining top and bottom.

Back
Row 1: Ch 13, sc in second ch from hook, sc in each ch across, turn. *(12 sc made)*
Rows 2–20: Ch 1, sc in each st across, turn. At end of last row, fasten off.
Using Back as pattern, cut piece from plastic canvas ⅛" smaller on all edges for lining back.

Front
Row 1: Ch 13, sc in second ch from hook, sc in each ch across, turn. *(12 sc made)*
Rows 2–34: Ch 1, sc in each st across, turn. At end of last row, fasten off.
With yarn, whipstitch *(see illustration)* short ends of two sheets of plastic canvas together.

Using Front as pattern, center over plastic canvas pieces, cut piece ⅛" smaller on all edges for lining front.

Top
Row 1: Ch 23, sc in second ch from hook, sc in each ch across, turn. *(22 sc made)*
Rows 2–3: Ch 1, sc in each st across, turn.
Rows 4–5: Ch 1, sc first 2 sts tog, sc in each st across to last 2 sts, sc last 2 sts tog, turn. At end of last row *(18)*.
Rows 6–8: Ch 1, sc in each st across, turn.
Rows 9–14: Ch 1, sc first 2 sts tog, sc in each st across to last 2 sts, sc last 2 sts tog, turn. At end of last row, fasten off. *(6)*
Row 15: Join with sc in end of row 1, sc in end of each row and in each st around to opposite end of row 1. Fasten off.

Strap
Row 1: Ch 5, sc in second ch from hook, sc in each ch across, turn. *(4 sc made)*
Rows 2–90: Ch 1, sc in each st across, turn. At end of last row, fasten off.

Button Loop
Ch 12. Fasten off. Sew ends to center front edge of Top.

Finishing
1: Matching sts, sl st Front and Back together. Sl st Bottom in place. Sl st straight edge of Top to ends of rows on Back.
2: With yarn, whipstitch front, back and bottom lining pieces together. Whipstitch straight edge of lining top to top straight edge of lining back. Insert lining into Basket. Tack in place.
3: Sew Strap ends to each side of Basket.
4: Sew fly to top of Basket.
5: Sew one end of lure to center Front of Basket behind Button Loop. Pull lure through Button Loop. ♥

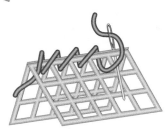

Ring Bearer's Pillow

Designed by Liz Eads

Finished Size: 12" across.

Materials:
- ❑ 6 oz. white pompadour baby yarn
- ❑ 12" × 24" piece white satin
- ❑ 4 yds. white ¼" picot ribbon
- ❑ 7½" spray of silk flowers
- ❑ Silver 6mm tinsel stem
- ❑ Polyester fiberfill
- ❑ White sewing thread
- ❑ Sewing needle
- ❑ D hook or hook needed to obtain gauge

Gauge: Rnds 1–3 are 1½" across.

Basic Stitches: Ch, sl st, sc, dc.

Side (make 2)
Rnd 1: Ch 2, 6 sc in second ch from hook, **do not join.** *(6 sc made)*

Rnd 2: 2 sc in each st around, join with sl st in first sc. *(12)*

Rnd 3: Ch 4, (dc in next st, ch 1) around, join with sl st in third ch of ch-4. *(12 dc) First 3 chs of ch-4 count as first dc.*

Rnd 4: Ch 3, 2 dc in first ch sp, (dc in next st, 2 dc in next ch sp) around, join with sl st in top of ch-3. *(36)*

Rnd 5: Ch 1, sc in first st, ch 3, skip next st, (sc in next st, ch 3, skip next st) around, join.

Rnds 6–7: (Sl st, ch 1, sc) in first ch sp, ch 3, (sc in next ch sp, ch 3) around, join.

Rnd 8: For **beginning shell (beg shell), (sl st, ch 3, dc, ch 2, 2 dc) in first ch sp;** ch 3, sc in next ch sp, ch 3; for **shell, *(2 dc, ch 2, 2 dc) in next ch sp;** ch 3, sc in next ch sp, ch 3; repeat from * around, join with sl st in top of ch-3. *(9 shells)*

Rnd 9: Sl st in next st, beg shell, ch 3, (sc in next ch sp, ch 3) 2 times, *shell in ch sp of next shell, ch 3, (sc in next ch sp, ch 3) 2 times; repeat from * around, join.

Rnd 10: Sl st in next st, (sl st, ch 3, 6 dc) in next ch sp, ch 3, skip next ch sp, dc in next ch sp, ch 3, skip next ch sp, (7 dc in next shell, ch 3, skip next ch sp, dc in next ch sp, ch 3, skip next ch sp) around, join.

Rnd 11: Ch 4, dc in next st, (ch 1, dc in next st) 5 times, ch 3, skip next ch sp, sc in next st, ch 3, skip next ch sp, *dc in next st, (ch 1, dc in next st) 6 times, ch 3, skip next ch sp, sc in next st, ch 3, skip next ch sp; repeat from * around, join with sl st in third ch of ch-4.

Rnd 12: (Sl st, ch 1, sc) in first ch sp, (ch 3, sc in next ch sp) 5 times, ch 5, skip next 3 sts and next 2 ch sps, *sc in next ch sp, (ch 3, sc in next ch sp) 5 times, ch 5, skip next 3 sts and next 2 ch sps; repeat from * around, join with sl st in first sc.

Rnds 13–16: (Sl st, ch 1, sc) in first ch sp, ch 3, (sc in next ch sp, ch 3) around, join. At end of last rnd, fasten off.

Pillow Form
Using crochet side as pattern, from satin, cut two pieces ¾" larger around outer edge. Allowing ¼" for seam, sew pieces right sides together leaving 2" open for turning. Turn right side out. Stuff. Sew opening closed.

Ruffle
Rnd 1: Hold Pillow Sides with wrong sides together, matching ch sps; working in ch sps through both thicknesses, join with sc in any ch sp, 3 sc in same ch sp, 4 sc in each ch sp around, inserting Pillow Form before closing, join with sl st in first sc.

Rnd 2: Ch 1, sc in first st, ch 3, (sc in next st, ch 3) around, join.

Rnds 3–5: (Sl st, ch 1, sc) in first ch sp, ch 3, (sc in next ch sp, ch 3) around, join. At end of last rnd, fasten off.

Finishing
Cut six pieces ribbon each 24" long. With all pieces held together, fold in half, tack folded ends to 7 dc group of rnd 10 on one Pillow Side. Tack flowers to Pillow, covering folded ends of ribbon.

For rings, cut two pieces from tinsel stem each 2½" long. Bend one piece to form circle, secure ends by twisting together. Repeat with other piece. Tie two pieces of ribbon in bow around each ring *(see photo).* ♥

Love
bears all thing
believe's all thing

Love
hopes all thing
endures all things,

Love
never ends . . .
Corinthians 13:7-8

Baby Powder Baby

Designed by Elizabeth Ann White

Finished Size: About 14½" tall *(fits over 8½"-tall × 3"-wide container of baby powder).*

Materials:
- ❑ 400 yds. white size 10 crochet cotton thread
- ❑ 3 small ribbon roses
- ❑ 1¼ yd. of ¼" ribbon
- ❑ 2" craft teddy bear
- ❑ 4" piece of ⅜" wooden dowel painted white
- ❑ Polyester fiberfill
- ❑ Hot glue gun and glue
- ❑ White sewing thread and sewing needle
- ❑ No. 7 steel hook or hook needed to obtain gauge

Gauge: 8 dc = 1"; 4 dc rows = 1".

Basic Stitches: Ch, sl st, sc, dc, tr.

Head & Body

Rnd 1: Starting at top of Head, ch 4, sl st in first ch to form ring, ch 3 *(counts as dc)*, 11 dc in ring, join with sl st in top of ch-3. *(12 dc made)*

Rnd 2: (Ch 3, dc) in first st, 2 dc in each st around, join. *(24)*

Rnd 3: Ch 3, 2 dc in next st, (dc in next st, 2 dc in next st) around, join. *(36)*

Rnd 4: Ch 3, dc in next st, 2 dc in next st, (dc in each of next 2 sts, 2 dc in next st) around, join. *(48)*

Rnds 5–10: Ch 3, dc in each st around, join.

Rnd 11: Ch 3, dc in next st, dc next 2 sts tog, (dc in each of next 2 sts, dc next 2 sts tog) around, join. *(36)*

Rnd 12: Ch 3, dc next 2 sts tog, (dc in next st, dc next 2 sts tog) around, join. Stuff. *(24)*

Rnd 13: For **neck,** ch 2, dc in next st, (dc next 2 sts tog) around, skip ch-2, join with sl st in next dc. *(12)*

Rnd 14: Ch 3, dc in each st around, join with sl st in top of ch-3.

Rnd 15: For **body,** (ch 3, dc) in first st, 2 dc in each st around, join. *(24)*

Rnd 16: Ch 3, 2 dc in next st, (dc in next st, 2 dc in next st) around, join. *(36)*

Rnd 17: Ch 3, dc in next st, 2 dc in next st, (dc in each of next 2 sts, 2 dc in next st) around, join. *(48)*

Rnds 18–22: Ch 3, dc in each st around, join. At end of last rnd, fasten off.

Base

Rnds 1–4: Repeat rnds 1–4 of Head & Body. At end of last rnd, fasten off.

Insert dowel inside Body and Neck with dowel extended slightly into stuffing inside Head. Stuff Body around dowel.

Sl st or sew Base to last rnd on Body.

Gown

Row 1: Starting at neckline, ch 21, dc in fourth ch from hook, 2 dc in each ch across, turn. *(36 dc made)*

Rows 2–3: Ch 3, 2 dc in next st, (dc in next st, 2 dc in next st) across, turn. *(54, 81)*

Row 4: Ch 3, dc in each st across, turn.

Row 5: Ch 5 *(counts as dc and ch-2)*, skip next st, dc in next st, (ch 2, skip next st, dc in next st) across, turn. *(41 dc, 40 ch sps)*

Row 6: Ch 3, (3 dc in next ch sp, dc in next st) 5 times; for **Armhole,** skip next 10 ch sps; dc in next st, (3 dc in next ch sp, dc in next st) 10 times; for **Armhole,** skip next 10 ch sps; dc in next st, (3 dc in next ch sp, dc in next st) 5 times, turn. *(83 dc)*

Rnd 7: Working in rnds, ch 3, dc in each st around, join with sl st in top of ch-3, **do not turn.** *Joining is back of Gown.*

Rnds 8–40: Ch 3, dc in each st around, join.

Rnd 41: Ch 5, skip next 2 sts, dc in next st, (ch 2, skip next 2 sts, dc in next st) 26 times, ch 2, skip last st, join with sl st in third ch of ch-5. *(28 dc, 28 ch sps)*

Rnd 42: (Sl st, ch 5, dc) in first ch sp, ch 1, *(dc, ch 2, dc) in next ch sp, ch 1; repeat from * around, join.

Rnd 43: Skipping ch-1 sps; ch 1, sc in first ch-2 sp, ch 1, (tr, ch 1) 5 times in next ch-2 sp, *sc in next ch-2 sp, ch 1, (tr, ch 1) 5 times in next ch-2 sp; repeat from * around, join with sl st in first sc.

Rnd 44: Ch 1, *sc in next ch-1 sp, (ch 3, sc in next ch-1 sp) 5 times; repeat from * around, join. Fasten off.

Right Sleeve

Rnd 1: With Head toward you and back of Gown at right, join with sl st in last worked dc before Armhole, ch 3, (3 dc in next ch sp, dc in next st) 10 times, join with sl st in top of ch-3. *(41 dc made)*

Rnds 2–12: Ch 3, dc in each st around, join.

Rnds 13–14: Ch 2, (dc next 2 sts tog) around, join with sl st in top of ch-2. *(21, 11)*

Rnds 15–16: Ch 3, dc in each st around, join with sl st in top of ch-3.

Rnd 17: Ch 1, sc in first st, ch 3, (sc in next st, ch

continued on page 26

Baby Powder Baby

continued from page 24

3) around, join with sl st in first sc. Fasten off.

Left Sleeve
Rnds 1–17: With Head toward you and Front of Gown at left; repeat rnds 1–17 of Right Sleeve.

Hand (make 2)
Note: Work in continuous rnds; do not join or turn. Mark first st of each rnd.
Rnd 1: Ch 2, 6 sc in second ch from hook. *(6 sc made)*
Rnd 2: 2 sc in each st around. *(12)*
Rnd 3: Sc in each st around.
Rnds 4–5: (Sc next 2 sts tog) around. *(6, 3)* At end of last rnd, fasten off.
Sew rnd 5 of Hands to each Sleeve at wrist.

Yoke Ruffle
Row 1: With Head toward you, join with **sc front post** *(fp, see Stitch Guide)* around post of last st on row 5 of Gown, (ch 4, sc fp around post of next st) across, turn. *(40 ch sps made)*
Rnd 2: (Sl st, ch 5, dc) in first ch sp, *ch 1, (dc, ch 2, dc) in next ch sp; repeat from * around, join with sl st in third ch of ch-5.
Rnd 3: Skipping ch-1 sps, ch 1, sc in first ch-2 sp, ch 1, (tr, ch 1) 5 times in next ch-2 sp, *sc in next ch-2 sp, ch 1, (tr, ch 1) 5 times in next ch-2 sp; repeat from * around, join with sl st in first sc.
Rnd 4: Ch 1, *sc in next ch-1 sp, (ch 3, sc in next ch-1 sp) 5 times; repeat from * around, join. Fasten off.

Bonnet
Row 1: Starting at back, ch 25, sl st in first ch to form ring, ch 5 *(counts as dc and ch-2)*, dc in ring, (ch 2, dc in ring) 12 times, turn. *(14 dc, 13 ch sps made)*
Row 2: Ch 5, skip first ch sp, dc in next st, (3 dc in next ch sp) 11 times, dc in next st, ch 2, skip next 2 chs of ch-5, dc in next ch, turn. *(37 dc, 2 ch sps)*
Rows 3–5: Ch 5, skip first ch sp, dc in next 35

sts, ch 2, skip last ch sp, dc in last st, turn.
Row 6: Ch 5, skip first ch sp, dc in next st, (ch 2, skip next st, dc in next st) 17 times, ch 2, skip last ch sp, dc in last st, turn. *(20 dc, 19 ch sps)*
Row 7: (Sl st, ch 5, dc) in first ch sp, (dc, ch 2, dc) in each ch sp across, turn.
Row 8: Ch 1, sc in first ch sp, *ch 1, (tr, ch 1) 5 times in next ch sp, sc in next ch sp; repeat from * across, turn.
Row 9: Ch 1, *sc in next ch sp, (ch 3, sc in next ch sp) 5 times; repeat from * across. Fasten off.
Row 10: For **edging**, join with sc in end of row 6, 2 sc in same row, 3 sc in end of next 5 rows, 3 sc in center ring on row 1, 3 sc in end of next 6 rows. Fasten off.

Finishing
1: Stuff Sleeves. Place Gown on Body; sew back opening closed.
2: Cut one each 13½" long and one piece 24" long from ribbon.
3: Starting at back of Gown, weave 13½" ribbon through ch sps on row 5 tacking ends under at back. Glue one ribbon rose to center front of Gown on ribbon at Yoke.
4: Starting at front of Gown on left-hand side, weave 24" ribbon through ch sps on rnd 41. Tie in bow.
5: Glue Hands to each side of teddy bear.
6: For **Bonnet Tie,** cut two pieces each 9" long from ribbon.
7: Starting at center back of Crown, fold ¼" of one end on one 9" ribbon around stitch at one end of row 1 on Bonnet and tack in place,
8: Cut one piece 4½" and one piece 7½" long from ribbon.
9: Weave 4½" ribbon through sts of row 1; fold ends to wrong side and tack in place.
10: Weave 7½" ribbon through sts of row 6; fold ends to wrong side and tack in place.
11: Glue one ribbon rose to each end of row 6 over ribbon.
12: Place Bonnet on Head and tie in place. ♥

Crochet Christmas

Chapter Two — Quick Crochet Creations for Christmas!

If you love crochet as much as I do, then no doubt you also love to crochet for our favorite holiday —Christmas—as well! There's nothing that says love more than a gift that is given from the heart and made with your own two hands!

Elegant Ornaments

Designed by Carol Allen

No. 3

No. 5

No. 2

No. 4

No. 1

Basic Ornament

Materials For Each:
- ❑ 175 yds. white size 10 crochet cotton
- ❑ 10" of ⅜"-wide white velvet ribbon
- ❑ One red 25mm ribbon rose
- ❑ Pearl-head straight pins for decoration
- ❑ 2½" diameter red satin ball ornament
- ❑ 12" of gold No. 16 metallic braid
- ❑ Fabric glue
- ❑ No. 7 steel hook

Basic Stitches: Ch, sl st, sc, hdc, dc, tr, dtr.

Special Stitches: For **beginning treble cluster (beg tr cl),** sl st in first ch sp, ch 4, *yo 2 times, insert hook in same ch sp, yo, pull through sp, (yo, pull through 2 lps on hook) 2 times; repeat from * 2 more times, yo, pull through all lps on hook.

For **treble cluster (tr cl),** yo 2 times, insert hook in next ch sp, yo, pull through ch sp, (yo, pull through 2 lps on hook) 2 times, *yo 2 times, insert hook in same ch sp, yo, pull through sp, (yo, pull through 2 lps on hook) 2 times; repeat from * 2 more times, yo, pull through all lps on hook.

Finishing
To attach Cover to satin ball, place Cover over satin ball and insert ring through center of rnd 1; insert pearl-head straight pins through the Cover and into the ball in desired arrangement.

Tie ribbon in bow and tie to ring at top of satin ball with gold metallic braid.

Glue rose to center of bow.

Ornament 1

Cover
Rnd 1: Ch 6, sl st in first ch to form ring, ch 1, (sc, ch 3) 6 times in ring, join with sl st in first sc. *(6 ch sps made)*

Rnd 2: Beg tr cl *(see Special Stitches)*, ch 12, (**tr cl** in next ch sp, ch 12) around, join with sl st in top of beg tr cl.

Rnd 3: (Ch 1, sc, ch 5, sc) in beg tr cl, 7 sc in first ch sp; for **center point, ch 8, sl st in 7th ch from hook, (ch 9, sl st, ch 7, sl st) in same ch as last sl st;** 7 sc in same ch sp as last sc, *(sc, ch 5, sc) in next tr cl, 7 sc in next ch sp, work center point, 7 sc in same ch sp; repeat from * around, join with sl st in first sc. Fasten off.

Ornament 2

Cover
Rnd 1: Ch 6, sl st in first ch to form ring, ch 1, (sc, ch 3) 5 times in ring, ch 2, join with dc in first sc. *(Ch-2 and dc is joining ch sp) (6 ch sps made)*

Rnd 2: Ch 1, sc in joining ch sp, (ch 10, sc in next ch sp) around, ch 3, join with dtr in first sc. *(Ch-3 and joining dtr is joining ch sp)*

Rnd 3: Ch 1, (sc, ch 5, sc) in joining ch sp; for **center point, ch 7, sc in 4th ch from hook, (ch 3, sc in same ch) 2 times, ch 3;** (sc, ch 5, sc) in same ch sp, *ch 7, (sc, ch 5, sc) in next ch sp, work center point, (sc, ch 5, sc) in same ch sp; repeat from * 4 more times, ch 7, join with sl st in first sc. Fasten off.

Ornament 3

Cover
Rnd 1: Ch 6, sl st in first ch to form ring, ch 1, (sc, ch 4) 8 times in ring, join with sl st in first sc. *(8 ch sps made)*

Rnd 2: Beg tr cl *(see Special Stitches)* in first ch sp, ch 5, (**tr cl** in next ch sp, ch 5) around, join with sl st in top of beg tr cl.

Rnd 3: Ch 1; for **shell, (sc, 2 hdc, 2 dc, ch 4, sl st in 4th ch from hook, 2 dc, 2 hdc, sc)** in first ch sp, *4 sc in next ch sp, (ch 7; for **picot, sc in 4th ch from hook)** 4 times, sl st in same ch as 3rd picot made, ch 7, picot, sl st in same ch as first picot made, ch 3, 4 sc in same ch sp, shell in next ch sp; repeat from * 2 more times, 4 sc in last ch sp, (ch 7, picot) 4 times, sl st in same ch as 3rd picot made, ch 7, picot, sl st in same ch as first picot made, ch 3, 4 sc in same ch sp, join with sl st in first sc. Fasten off.

Ornament 4

Cover
Rnd 1: Ch 6, sl st in first ch to form ring, ch 1, (sc, ch 4) 5 times in ring, sc in ring, ch 1, join with dc in first sc. *(Ch-1 and dc is joining ch sp) (6 ch sps made)*

Rnd 2: Ch 1, sc in joining ch sp, ch 5, sc in same ch sp, *ch 2, (sc, ch 5, sc) in next ch sp; repeat from * 4 more times, ch 1, join with sc in first sc *(ch-1 and sc is joining ch sp).*

Rnd 3: Ch 1, sc in joining ch sp, ch 1, (*sc in next ch sp, ch 7, sc in same ch sp, ch 8, sc in same ch sp; for **center point, ch 13, sl st in 4th ch from hook, ch 9;** sc in same ch sp, ch 8, sc in same ch sp, ch 7, sc in same ch sp, ch 1*, sc in next ch sp, ch 1) 5 times; repeat between first and second *, join with sl st in first sc. Fasten off.

Ornament 5

Cover
Rnd 1: Ch 6, sl st in first ch to form ring, ch 1, (sc, ch 4) 5 times in ring, sc in ring, ch 1, join with dc in first sc. *(Ch-1 and dc is joining ch sp—6 ch sps made.)*

continued on page 32

Snowman Hot Pad

Designed by Michele Wilcox

Finished Size: Approximately 13½" tall.

Materials:
- ❑ Worsted yarn:
  - 3½ oz. white
  - 2 oz. red
  - 1 oz. black
  - ½ oz. med. green
  - Small amount dk. peach
- ❑ Tapestry needle
- ❑ F hook or hook needed to obtain gauge

Gauge: 9 sc = 2"; 9 sc rows = 2".

Basic Stitches: Ch, sl st, sc.

Note: When **changing colors** *(see Stitch Guide),* drop first color to wrong side of work, pick up next color. Always change colors in last st made.

Head & Body (make 2)
Row 1: With white, beginning at bottom, ch 13, sc in second ch from hook, sc in each ch across, turn. *(12 sc made)*
Rows 2–8: Ch 1, 2 sc in first st, sc in each st across to last st, 2 sc in last st, turn. *(26)*
Rows 9–20: Ch 1, sc in each st across, turn.
Rows 21–27: Ch 1, sc first 2 sts tog, sc in each st across to last st, sc last 2 sts tog, turn. *(12)*
Rows 28–31: Ch 1, 2 sc in first st, sc in each st across to last st, 2 sc in last st, turn. *(20)*
Rows 32–35: Ch 1, sc in each st across changing to red in last st made *(see Notes).* Fasten off white.
Rows 36–39: For **Hat,** ch 1, sc in each st across, turn.
Rows 40–41: Ch 1, sc first 2 sts tog, sc in each st across to last 2 sts, sc last 2 sts tog, turn. *(16)*
Row 42: Ch 1, sc in each st across, turn.
Rows 43–47: Ch 1, sc first 2 sts tog, sc in each st across to last 2 sts, sc last 2 sts tog, turn. At end of last row, fasten off. *(6)*

Facial Features (on one side only)
For **eyes,** with black embroider two satin stitches *(see Stitch Guide)* 1½" apart over rows 33 and 34.
For **mouth,** with black embroider fly stitch *(see Stitch Guide)* over rows 30 and 31.
For **nose,** with dk. peach, embroider French knot *(see Stitch Guide)* between rows 32 and 33 between eyes.

Assembly
With wrong sides together and front facing you, working through both thicknesses, using matching colors, join with sc in first ch on opposite side of starting ch, sc in each ch, in end of each row and in each st around with 2 sc at curves where needed to keep work flat.

Hat Cuff
Row 1: With red, ch 6, sc in second ch from hook, sc in each ch across, turn. *(5 sc made)*
Rows 2–22: Working in **back lps** *(see Stitch Guide),* ch 1, sc in each st across, turn. At end of last row, fasten off.
Sew ends of rows on one edge of Cuff to row 36 of Hat. Sew first and last row and opposite edge of Cuff to Hat.

Scarf (make 2)
Row 1: With med. green, ch 21, sc in second ch from hook, sc in each ch across, turn. *(20 sc made)*
Rows 2–3: Ch 1, sc in each st across, turn. At end of last row, fasten off.
Place one Scarf piece centered over second piece *(see facial features illustration).* Sew one end of Scarf piece to each side at neck, tacking edges and remaining ends to Body.

Arm (make 4)
Row 1: Starting at top edge, with white, ch 9, sc in second ch from hook, sc in each ch across, turn. *(8 sc made)*
Rows 2–8: Ch 1, sc in each st across, turn.
Rows 9–10: Ch 1, sc first 2 sts tog, sc in each st across to last 2 sts, sc last 2 sts tog, turn. At end of last row, fasten off. *(4)*
Match ends of rows on two Arm pieces together; working through both thicknesses, join white with sc in end of row 1, sc in end of each row and in each st across ending at opposite side of row 1. Fasten off leaving top edge unworked. Repeat with other Arm pieces.
Sew one Arm to each side of Body below Scarf.

Boot (make 4)
Row 1: Starting at bottom, with black, ch 12, sc in second ch from hook, sc in each ch across, turn. *(11 sc made)*
Rows 2–4: Ch 1, sc in each st across, turn.
Row 5: Ch 1, sc first 2 sts tog, sc in each st across, turn. *(10)*

continued on page 32

continued from page 29

Rnd 2: Ch 1, sc in joining ch sp; for **point,** ch 4, sc in second ch from hook, sc in next 2 ch; sc in same ch sp, (ch 4, sc in next ch sp; for **point,** ch 4, sc in second ch from hook, sc in next 2 ch; sc in same ch sp) around, ch 1, join with dc in first sc.

Rnd 3: Ch 1, 2 sc in joining ch sp, ch 4, sc in ch at top of first point, ch 7, sl st in 7th ch from hook, sc in same ch at top of point, ch 11, sl st in 5th ch from hook, (ch 4, sl st in same ch) 2 times, sc in next 6 ch of ch 11, sc in same ch at top of first point, ch 7, sl st in 7th ch from hook, sc in same ch at top of point, ch 4, *2 sc in next ch sp, ch 4, sc in ch at top of next point, ch 7, sl st in 7th ch from hook, sc in same ch at top of point, ch 11, sl st in 5th ch from hook, (ch 4, sl st in same ch) 2 times, sc in next 6 ch of ch 11, sc in same ch at top of point, ch 7, sl st in 7th ch from hook, sc in same ch at top of point, ch 4; repeat from * around, join with sl st in first sc. Fasten off. ❄

Snowman Hot Pad

continued from page 30

Row 6: Ch 1, sc in each st across to last 2 sts, sc last 2 sts tog, turn. *(9)*

Rows 7–8: Repeat rows 5 and 6. *(7)*

Rows 9–13: Ch 1, sc in each st across, turn. At end of last row, fasten off.

Match ends of rows on two Boot pieces together; working through both thicknesses, join black with sc in end of row 13, sc in end of each row and on opposite side of starting ch across ending at opposite end of row 13. Fasten off leaving top edge unworked. Repeat with other Boot pieces.

Sew top edge of each Boot to bottom of Body 1½" apart. ❄

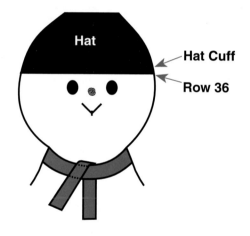

Granny Square Earrings

Designed by Debra Woodard

Finished Size: Approximately $1\frac{5}{8}$" × $2\frac{3}{8}$" without wire.

Materials:
- ❑ Small amount each red, green and white size 10 crochet cotton thread
- ❑ One pair kidney wires
- ❑ Embroidery needle
- ❑ No. 9 steel hook or hook needed to obtain gauge

Gauge: Square = $\frac{3}{4}$" across.

Basic Stitches: Ch, sl st, sc.

Earring (make 2)
Square (make 4)
Rnd 1: With red, ch 3, sl st in first ch to form ring, ch 1, (3 sc in ring, ch 2) 4 times, join with sl st in first sc. Fasten off. *(4 ch sps made)*

Rnd 2: Join green with sc in any ch sp, (sc, ch 2, 2 sc) in same ch sp, ch 1, *(2 sc, ch 2, 2 sc) in next ch sp, ch 1; repeat from * around, join. Fasten off. *(8 ch sps)*

Rnd 3: Join white with sc in any ch-2 sp, (sc, ch 1, 2 sc) in same ch sp, *ch 1, 2 sc in next ch-1 sp, ch 1, (2 sc, ch 1, 2 sc) in next ch-2 sp; repeat from *. 2 more times, ch 1, 2 sc in last ch-1 sp, ch 1, join. Fasten off.

Working in **back lps** *(see Stitch Guide)*, sew Squares together according to illustration. *(Use the assemly illustration that pertains to the side you are working.)*

Edging

For **each Earring**, working in **back lps**, join red with sc in ch at top back corner *(see dot on illustration)*, ch 3, sc in same ch *(loop made)*, sc in each st and in each ch and in each seam around, join with sl st in first sc. Fasten off.

Insert wires through loops on Earrings. ✸

Christmas Wreath

Designed by Susie Spier Maxfield

Finished Size: 12" across.

Materials:
- ❑ 7 oz. green worsted yarn
- ❑ 10" straw wreath
- ❑ 9" red Christmas bow
- ❑ Decorative Christmas picks
- ❑ 7" gold Christmas tinsel trim
- ❑ Floral T-pins
- ❑ 2 large bells
- ❑ Tapestry needle
- ❑ H hook or hook needed to obtain gauge

Gauge: 3 sc = 1"; 2 sc rows = 1".

Basic Stitches: Ch, sl st, sc.

Special Stitch:

For **loop stitch (lp st**—*see illustration),* insert hook in st, wrap yarn 2 times around finger, insert hook from left to right through all lps on finger, pull lps through st, drop lps from finger, yo, pull through all lps on hook.

Cover

Rnd 1: Ch 65, sl st in first ch to form ring, ch 1, sc in first ch, (2 sc in next ch, sc in next ch) around, join with sl st in first sc. *(97 sc made)*

Rnd 2: Ch 1, sc in each st around, join.

Rnds 3–12: Ch 1, **lp st** *(see Special Stitch)* in each st around, join with sl st in first lp st.

Rnds 13–14: Ch 1, sc in each st around, join with sl st in first sc. Fasten off.

Place Cover over wreath, sew first and last rnds together.

Wrap 7" gold tinsel trim around center of bow; twist ends together to secure. Insert one end of gold trim through opening on each bell, twist ends together to secure.

Using floral T-pins, decorate wreath as desired with Christmas picks and bow. ❉

Bible Cover

Designed by Julie Tackitt

Finished Size: Fits 7" × 9½" Bible.

Materials:
- ❑ Worsted yarn:
    - 8 oz. peach
    - 4 oz. white
- ❑ Tapestry needle
- ❑ H hook or hook needed to obtain gauge

Gauge: 13 sc = 3"; 10 sc rows = 2".

Basic Stitches: Ch, sl st, sc, dc.

Cover
Row 1: With peach, ch 41, sc in second ch from hook, sc in each ch across, turn. *(40 sc made)*
Rows 2–72: Ch 1, sc in each st across, turn. At end of last row, fasten off.

Flap (make 2)
Row 1: With peach, ch 41, sc in second ch from hook, sc in each ch across, turn. *(40 sc made)*
Rows 2–26: Ch 1, sc in each st across, turn. At end of last row, fasten off.

Pencil Pocket
Row 1: With peach, ch 31, sc in second ch from hook, sc in each ch across, turn. *(30 sc made)*
Rows 2–12: Ch 1, sc in each st across, turn. At end of last row, fasten off.

Front Pocket
Row 1: With peach, ch 31, sc in second ch from hook, sc in each ch across, turn. *(30 sc made)*
Note: *When **changing colors** (see Stitch Guide), drop first color to back side of work, pick up next color. Always change colors in last st made.*
Row 2: Ch 1, sc in first 16 sts changing to white in last st made *(see Note),* sc in each of next 2 sts changing to peach, sc in each st across, turn. *Front of row 2 is right side of work.*
Row 3: Ch 1, sc in first 11 sts changing to white, sc in next 4 sts changing to peach, sc in each st across, turn.
Row 4: Ch 1, sc in first 14 sts changing to white, sc in next 6 sts changing to peach, sc in each st across, turn.
Row 5: Ch 1, sc in first 10 sts changing to white, sc in next 6 sts changing to peach, sc in each st across, turn.
Row 6: Ch 1, sc in first 14 sts changing to white, sc in next 6 sts changing to peach, sc in each st across, turn.
Row 7: Ch 1, sc in first 11 sts changing to white, sc in next 4 sts changing to peach, sc in each st across, turn.
Row 8: Ch 1, sc in first 15 sts changing to white, sc in next 4 sts changing to peach, sc in each st across, turn.
Row 9: Ch 1, sc in first 11 sts changing to white, sc in next 4 sts changing to peach, sc in each st across, turn.
Row 10: Ch 1, sc in each of first 3 sts changing to white, sc in each of next 3 sts changing to peach, sc in next 9 sts changing to white, sc in next 4 sts changing to peach, sc in next 5 sts changing to white, sc in each of next 3 sts changing to peach, sc in each st across, turn.
Row 11: Ch 1, sc in each of first 2 sts changing to white, sc in next 26 sts changing to peach, sc in each st across, turn.
Rows 12–13: Ch 1, sc in first st changing to white, sc in next 28 sts changing to peach, sc in each st across, turn.
Row 14: Ch 1, sc in each of first 2 sts changing to white, sc in next 26 sts changing to peach, sc in each st across, turn.
Row 15: Ch 1, sc in each of first 3 sts changing to white, sc in each of next 3 sts changing to peach, sc in each st across, turn.
Row 16: Ch 1, sc in first 15 sts changing to white, sc in next 4 sts changing to peach, sc in each st across, turn.
Row 17: Ch 1, sc in first 11 sts changing to white, sc in next 4 sts changing to peach, sc in each st across, turn.
Row 18: Ch 1, sc in first 15 sts changing to white, sc in next 4 sts changing to peach, sc in each st across turn.
Row 19: Ch 1, sc in first 10 sts changing to white, sc in next 6 sts changing to peach, sc in each st across, turn.
Row 20: Ch 1, sc in first 14 sts changing to white, sc in next 6 sts changing to peach, sc in each st across, turn.
Row 21: Ch 1, sc in first 10 sts changing to white, sc in next 6 sts changing to peach, sc in each st across, turn.
Row 22: Ch 1, sc in first 15 sts changing to white, sc in next 4 sts changing to peach, sc in each st across, turn.
Row 23: Ch 1, sc in first 12 sts changing to white, sc in next 2 sts changing to peach, sc in each st across, turn.
Row 24: Ch 1, sc in each st across, turn.
Rnd 25: Working around outer edge, ch 1, sc in each st and in end of each row around with 3 sc in each corner, join with sl st in first sc, turn. Fasten off. *(116 sc)*
Rnd 26: Join white with sc in center st of first 3-sc group at corner, 2 sc in same st as last sc, sc in each st around with 3 sc in center st of 3-sc group at corner, join. *(124)*
Rnd 27: For **ruffle**, ch 1, (sc, ch 3, dc) in first st, *skip next 2 sts, (sc, ch 3, dc) in next st; repeat from * 29 more times, sl st in next st leaving remaining sts unworked for opening. Fasten off.

Handle (make 2)
Row 1: With peach, ch 43, sc in second ch from continued on page 44

Chenille Ornaments

Designed by Elizabeth Ann White

Instructions begin on page 40

Chenille Ornaments

Photo on pages 38 & 39

Heart Ornament

Finished Size: 6" × 6" excluding hanger.

Materials:
- ❏ 50 yds. red chenille sport yarn
- ❏ 50 yds. gold/gold size 10 metallic crochet cotton thread
- ❏ 5" square 7-mesh plastic canvas
- ❏ 10" gold metallic ⅛" ribbon
- ❏ Red sewing thread
- ❏ Sewing needle
- ❏ No. 0 and No. 5 steel hooks or hooks needed to obtain gauges

Gauges: With No. 0 hook and yarn, 5 dc = 1"; 2 dc rows = 1". **With No. 5 hook and thread,** Rose is 2" across.

Basic Stitches: Ch, sl st, sc, dc, tr.

Heart Side (make 2)
Row 1: Starting at **Point,** with No. 0 hook and red, ch 4, 4 dc in fourth ch from hook, turn. *(First 3 chs count as first dc — 5 dc made.)*
Row 2: (Ch 3, dc) in first st, 2 dc in next st, dc in next st, 2 dc in each of last 2 sts, turn. *(9)*
Rows 3–5: (Ch 3, dc) in first st, 2 dc in next st, dc in each st across to last 2 sts, 2 dc in each of last 2 sts, turn. *(21 sts at end of last row)*
Row 6: (Ch 3, dc) in first st, dc in each st across to last st, 2 dc in last st, turn. *(23)*
Rows 7–8: Ch 3, dc in each st across, turn.
Row 9: For **first side,** ch 2, dc next 2 sts tog, dc in next 6 sts, dc next 3 sts tog leaving last 11 sts unworked, turn.
Row 10: Ch 2, dc next 2 sts tog, dc in each of next 2 sts, dc next 3 sts tog leaving ch-2 unworked, **do not turn.** Fasten off.
Row 9: For **second side,** with No. 0 hook, join red with sl st in first st on opposite side of row 8, ch 2, dc next 2 sts tog, dc in next 6 sts, dc next 3 sts tog *(last st will be worked in same st as last st of row 9 on first side),* turn.
Row 10: Repeat row 10 of first side.
Using crochet piece as a pattern, cut plastic canvas.

Edging
Rnd 1: Hold Heart Sides together with plastic canvas between, matching sts; working through both thicknesses around outer edge in ends of rows and in sts, with No. 5 hook, join gold with sc in same st on row 8 that last st of row 9 was worked in, ch 5, evenly space (sc, ch 5) 18 times across to row 1, (sc, ch 5) in row 1, (sc, ch 5) 2 times in Point, sc in end of row 1, evenly space (ch 5, sc) 18 times across to inside end of row 9, ch 2, join with dc in first sc *(joining ch sp made),* turn. *(41 ch sps made)*
Row 2: Working in rows, ch 1, sc in joining ch sp, (ch 5, sc in next ch sp) 19 times, ch 5, (sc, ch 5, sc) in ch sp at Point of Heart, (ch 5, sc in next ch sp) 19 times, ch 2, dc in last ch sp, turn.
Row 3: Ch 1, sc in joining ch sp, (ch 5, sc in next ch sp) 19 times, ch 5, (sc, ch 5, sc) in ch sp at Point, (ch 5, sc in next ch sp) 20 times, **do not turn.**
Rnd 4: Working in ch sps around outer edge, ch 1, 3 sc in each of first 4 ch sps, (3 sc, ch 3, sl st in last sc made, 3 sc) in each ch sp around, join with sl st in first sc. Fasten off. *Front of rnd 4 is right side of work.*

Rose
Rnd 1: With No. 5 hook and gold, ch 4, sl st in first ch to form ring, ch 1, (sc, ch 3) 6 times in ring, join with sl st in first sc. *(6 sc, 6 ch-3 sps made)*
Rnd 2: For **petals,** ch 1, (sc, ch 1, 5 dc, ch 1, sc) in each ch-3 sp around, join. *(6 petals)*
Rnd 3: Working behind petals, ch 4, *sc in **back strands** *(see illustration)* of first sc on next petal, ch 3; repeat from * around, join with sl st in first ch of first ch-4.
Rnd 4: Ch 1, (sc, ch 1, 7 dc, ch 1, sc) in each ch-3 sp around, join with sl st in first sc.
Rnd 5: Working behind petals, ch 5, (sc in back strands of first sc on next petal, ch 4) around, join with sl st in first ch of first ch-5.
Rnd 6: Ch 1, (sc, ch 1, 4 dc, tr, 4 dc, ch 1, sc) in each ch-4 sp around, join with sl st in first sc. Fasten off.
With sewing needle and thread, sew Rose to front of Heart *(see photo).*
For **hanger,** fold ribbon in half; tack ends to back of Heart. ❅

Bolster Ornament

Finished Size: 8" long.

Materials:
- ❏ 50 yds. red chenille sport yarn
- ❏ 50 yds. gold/gold metallic size 10 crochet cotton thread
- ❏ 4½" × 7" square red fabric
- ❏ 60" gold metallic ⅛" ribbon
- ❏ 2 gold ribbon roses
- ❏ Polyester fiberfill
- ❏ Red sewing thread
- ❏ Sewing needle
- ❏ No. 0 and No. 5 steel hooks or hooks needed to obtain gauges

Gauges: With No. 0 hook and yarn, 5 dc = 1"; 2 dc rows = 1". **With No. 5 hook and thread,** Rose is 2" across.

Basic Stitches: Ch, sl st, sc, dc, tr.

Bolster
Row 1: With No. 0 hook and red, ch 36, dc in fourth ch from hook, dc in each of next 3 chs, ch 2, skip next 2 chs, dc in next 20 chs, ch 2, skip next 2 chs, dc in last 5 chs, turn. *(First 3 chs count as first dc — 30 dc, 2 ch sps made.)*

Rows 2–15: Ch 3, dc in next 4 sts, ch 2, skip next ch sp, dc in next 20 sts, ch 2, skip next ch sp, dc in last 5 sts, turn.

Matching sts, sl st row 15 to opposite side of starting ch to form a tube. Fasten off.

Edging
Rnd 1: Working in ends of rows on one end of Bolster, with No. 5 hook, join gold with sc in end of any row, (ch 5, sc, ch 5) in end of same row, (sc, ch 5) 2 times in end of each row around to last row, (sc, ch 5, sc, ch 2) in end of last row, join with dc in first sc *(joining ch sp made)*. *(30 ch sps made)*

Rnds 2–3: (Ch 1, sc) in joining ch sp, (ch 5, sc in next sp) around, ch 2, join with dc in first sc.

Rnd 4: (Ch 1, sc) in joining ch sp, (ch 5, sc in next sp) around, ch 5, join with sl st in first sc.

Rnd 5: Ch 1, (3 sc, ch 3, sl st in top of last sc made, 3 sc) in each ch sp around, join. Fasten off.

Repeat on other end of Bolster.

Rose
Work same as Heart Ornament Rose on page 40.

Finishing
1: For **form,** allowing ¼" for seam, sew 4½" ends of fabric together to form a tube. Turn right side out. Turn raw edges under ¼" to wrong side. Run a gathering thread around edges; stuffing before closing, pull thread to close. Insert form into crocheted piece.

2: Cut four pieces of ribbon each 12" long. With two pieces held together weave through ch sps on each end of Ornament; pull to close opening, tie in bow. Tack ribbon rose to center of each bow.

3: Sew Rose to center of Ornament *(see photo).*

4: For **hanger,** weave remaining ribbon under two sts three rows above Rose. Tie ends in knot. Trim. ❈

Round Ornament

Finished Size: 7" across.

Materials:
❑ 50 yds. red chenille sport yarn
❑ 50 yds. gold/gold metallic size 10 crochet cotton thread
❑ 5" square 7-mesh plastic canvas

❑ 12" gold metallic ⅛" ribbon
❑ Red sewing thread
❑ Sewing needle
❑ No. 0 and No. 5 steel hooks or hooks needed to obtain gauges

Gauges: **With No. 0 hook and yarn,** 5 dc = 1"; 2 dc rows = 1". **With No. 5 hook and thread,** Rose is 2" across.

Basic Stitches: Ch, sl st, sc, dc, tr.

Round Side (make 2)
Rnd 1: With No. 0 hook and red, ch 4, 11 dc in fourth ch from hook, join with sl st in top of ch-4. *(First 3 chs count as first dc — 12 dc made.)*

Rnd 2: (Ch 3, dc) in first st, 2 dc in each st around, join with sl st in top of ch-3. *(24)*

Rnd 3: (Ch 3, dc) in first st, dc in next st, (2 dc in next st, dc in next st) around, join. *(36)*

Rnd 4: (Ch 3, dc) in first st, dc in each of next 2 sts, (2 dc in next st, dc in each of next 2 sts) around, join. *(48)*

Rnd 5: (Ch 3, dc) in first st, dc in each of next 3 sts, (2 dc in next st, dc in each of next 3 sts) around, join. Fasten off. *(60)*

Using crocheted piece as a pattern, cut plastic canvas.

Edging
Rnd 1: Hold Round Sides together with plastic canvas between, matching sts; working through both thicknesses, with No. 5 hook, join gold with sc in any st, (ch 5, sc in next st) around, ch 2, join with dc in first sc *(joining ch sp made). (60 ch sps made)* Front of rnd 1 is right side of work.

Rnds 2–3: (Ch 1, sc) in joining ch sp, (ch 5, sc in next st) around, ch 2, join with dc in first sc.

Rnd 4: (Ch 1, sc) in joining ch sp, ch 5, (sc in next sp, ch 5) around, join with sl st in first sc.

Rnd 5: Ch 1, (3 sc, ch 3, sl st in top of last sc made, 3 sc) in each ch sp around, join. Fasten off.

Rose
Work same as Heart Ornament Rose on page 40. Sew Rose to center front of Ornament.

For **hanger,** weave ribbon through two ch sps on rnd 1 of Edging; tie ends in knot. ❈

Star Ornament

Finished Size: 7" across.

Materials:
❑ 50 yds. red chenille sport yarn

continued on page 42

Chenille Ornaments

continued from page 41

- ❏ 50 yds. gold/gold metallic size 10 crochet cotton thread
- ❏ 7" square 7-mesh plastic canvas
- ❏ Red sewing thread
- ❏ Sewing needle
- ❏ No. 0 and No. 5 steel hooks or hooks needed to obtain gauges

Gauges: **With No. 0 hook and yarn,** 5 dc = 1"; 2 dc rows = 1". **With No. 5 hook and thread,** Rose is 2" across.

Basic Stitches: Ch, sl st, sc, dc, tr.

Star Side (make 2)

Rnd 1: With No. 0 hook and red, ch 4, 9 dc in fourth ch from hook, join with sl st in top of ch-4. *(First 3 chs count as first dc — 10 dc made.)*

Rnd 2: (Ch 3, dc) in first st, 2 dc in each st around, join with sl st in top of ch-3. *(20)*

Rnd 3: (Ch 1, sc) in first st, skip next st, (3 dc, ch 2, 3 dc) in next st, skip next st, *sc in next st, skip next st, (3 dc, ch 2, 3 dc) in next st, skip next st; repeat from * around, join with sl st in first sc.

Rnd 4: Ch 1, dc in each of first 3 sts, (3 dc, ch 2, 3 dc) in ch-2 sp, *dc in each of next 3 sts, sl st in next st, dc in next 3 sts, (3 dc, ch 2, 3 dc) in ch-2 sp; repeat from * 3 more times, dc in each of last 3 sts, join with sl st in first ch-1.

Rnd 5: Ch 1, dc in first 6 sts, (3 dc, tr, 3 dc) in ch-2 sp, *dc in next 6 sts, ch 1, sl st in next sl st, ch 1, dc in next 6 sts, (3 dc, tr, 3 dc) in ch-2 sp; repeat from * 3 more times, dc in last 6 sts, ch 1, join with sl st in first ch-1. Fasten off.

Using crocheted piece as a pattern, cut plastic canvas.

Edging

Rnd 1: Hold Star Sides together with plastic canvas between, matching sts; working through both thicknesses, with No. 5 hook, join gold with sc in first ch-1 sp, *(ch 5, skip next st, sc in next st) 4 times, ch 5, (sc, ch 5, sc) in next tr, (ch 5, skip next st, sc in next st) 4 times, ch 5, sc in next 2 ch-1 sps; repeat from * 3 more times, (ch 5, skip next st, sc in next st) 4 times, ch 5, (sc, ch 5, sc) in next tr, (ch 5, skip next st, sc in next st) 4 times, ch 5, sc in last ch-1 sp, join with sl st in first sc. *Front of rnd 1 is right side of work.*

Rnd 2: Ch 1, (2 sc, ch 2, sl st in top of last sc made, 2 sc) in each ch sp around, join. Fasten off.

Rose

Work same as Heart Ornament Rose on page 40. Sew Rose to center front of Ornament.

For **hanger,** weave 12" piece of gold thread through two sts of rnd 1 on Edging at one point of Star. ❄

Square Ornament

Finished Size: 7" across.

Materials:
- ❏ 50 yds. red chenille sport yarn
- ❏ 50 yds. gold/gold metallic size 10 crochet cotton thread
- ❏ 4" square 7-mesh plastic canvas
- ❏ Red sewing thread
- ❏ Sewing needle
- ❏ No. 0 and No. 5 steel hooks or hooks needed to obtain gauges

Gauges: **With No. 0 hook and yarn,** 5 dc = 1"; 2 dc rows = 1". **With No. 5 hook and thread,** Rose is 2" across.

Basic Stitches: Ch, sl st, sc, dc, tr.

Square Side (make 2)

Rnd 1: With No. 0 hook and red, ch 4, sl st in first ch to form ring, ch 3, (2 dc, ch 2) in ring, (3 dc, ch 2) 3 times in ring, join with sl st in top of ch-4. *(First 3 chs count as first dc — 12 dc, 4 ch sps made.)*

Rnd 2: Ch 3, dc in each of next 2 sts, *(dc, tr, ch 2, tr, dc) in next ch sp, dc in each of next 3 sts, (2 dc, ch 2, 2 dc) in next ch sp*, dc in each of next 3 sts; repeat between first and second *, join.

Rnds 3–4: Ch 3, dc in each st across to first ch sp, *(dc, tr, ch 2, tr, dc) in ch sp, dc in each st across to next ch sp (2 dc, ch 2, 2 dc) in ch sp*, dc in each st across to next ch sp; repeat between first and second *, join. At end of last rnd, fasten off.

Using crocheted piece as a pattern, cut plastic canvas.

Edging

Rnd 1: Hold Square Sides together with plastic canvas between, matching sts; working through both thicknesses, with No. 5 hook, join gold with sc in any corner ch-2 sp, ch 5, sc in same sp, *ch 5, (sc in next st, ch 5) across to next corner ch sp, (sc, ch 5, sc) in ch sp; repeat from * 2 more times, (ch 5, sc in next st) across, ch 2, join with dc in first st *(joining ch sp made).* Front of rnd 1 is right side of work.

Rnd 2: Ch 1, sc in joining ch sp, ch 5, (sc, ch 5, sc) in corner sp, *(ch 5, sc in next ch sp) across to corner sp, (sc, ch 5, sc) in corner sp; repeat from * 2 more times, (ch 5, sc in next ch sp) 15 times, ch 2, join with dc in first sc.

Rnd 3: Ch 1, sc in joining ch sp, ch 5, (sc, ch 5) in each ch sp around with (sc, ch 5, sc) in each corner sp, join with sl st in first sc.

Rnd 4: Ch 1, (3 sc, ch 3, sl st in top of last sc made, 3 sc) in each ch sp around, join. Fasten off.

Rose

Work same as Heart Ornament Rose on page 40. Sew Rose to center front of Ornament.

For **hanger,** weave a 12" piece of gold thread through two sts on rnd 3 of Edging at one corner. ✿

Cornucopia

Finished Size: 6" long excluding Tassel.

Materials:
- ❑ 50 yds. red chenille sport yarn
- ❑ 75 yds. gold/gold metallic size 10 crochet cotton thread
- ❑ Red sewing thread
- ❑ Sewing needle
- ❑ No. 0 and No. 5 steel hooks or hooks needed to obtain gauges

Gauges: **With No. 0 hook and yarn,** 5 dc = 1"; 2 dc rows = 1". **With No. 5 hook and thread,** Rose is 2" across.

Basic Stitches: Ch, sl st, sc, dc, tr.

Cornucopia

Rnd 1: With No. 0 hook and red, ch 4, 7 dc in fourth ch from hook, join with sl st in top of ch-4. *(First 3 chs count as first dc — 8 dc made.)*

Rnd 2: (Ch 3, dc) in first st, dc in each of next 3 sts, 2 dc in next st, dc in each of last 3 sts, join. *(10)*

Rnd 3: (Ch 3, dc) in first st, dc in next 4 sts, 2 dc in next st, dc in last 4 sts, join. *(12)*

Rnd 4: (Ch 3, dc) in first st, dc in next 5 sts, 2 dc in next st, dc in last 5 sts, join. *(14)*

Rnd 5: (Ch 3, dc) in first st, dc in next 6 sts, 2 dc in next st, dc in last 6 sts, join. *(16)*

Rnd 6: (Ch 3, dc) in first st, dc in next 7 sts, 2 dc in next st, dc in last 7 sts, join. *(18)*

Rnd 7: (Ch 3, dc) in first st, dc in next 8 sts, 2 dc in next st, dc in last 8 sts, join. *(20)*

Rnd 8: (Ch 3, dc) in first st, dc in next 9 sts, 2 dc in next st, dc in last 9 sts, join. *(22)*

Rnd 9: (Ch 3, dc) in first st, dc in next 10 sts, 2 dc in next st, dc in last 10 sts, join. *(24)*

Rnd 10: (Ch 3, dc) in first st, dc in next 11 sts, 2 dc in next st, dc in last 11 sts, join. *(26)*

Rnd 11: (Ch 3, dc) in first st, dc in next 12 sts, 2 dc in next st, dc in last 12 sts, join. *(28)*

Rnd 12: (Ch 3, dc) in first st, dc in next 13 sts, 2 dc in next st, dc in last 13 sts, join. *(30)*

Rnd 13: (Ch 3, dc) in first st, dc in next 14 sts, 2 dc in next st, dc in last 14 sts, join. *(32)*

Rnd 14: (Ch 3, dc) in first st, dc in next 15 sts, 2 dc in next st, dc in last 15 sts, join. *(34)*

Rnd 15: (Ch 3, dc) in first st, dc in next 16 sts, 2 dc in next st, dc in last 16 sts, join. Fasten off. *(36)*

Rnd 16: For **edging,** join gold with sc in any st, (ch 5, sc in next st) around, ch 2, join with dc in first sc *(joining sp made).*

Rnds 17–18: Ch 1, sc in joining sp, (ch 5, sc in next ch sp) around, ch 2, join with dc in first sc.

Rnd 19: Ch 1, sc in joining sp, (ch 5, sc in next ch sp) around, ch 5, join with sl st in first sc.

Rnd 20: Ch 1, (3 sc, ch 3, sl st in last sc made, 3 sc) in each ch sp around, join. Fasten off.

Rose

Rnd 1: With No. 5 hook and gold, ch 4, sl st in first ch to form ring, ch 1, (sc, ch 3) 6 times in ring, join with sl st in first sc. *(6 sc, 6 ch-3 sps made)*

Rnd 2: For **petals,** ch 1, (sc, ch 1, 5 dc, ch 1, sc) in each ch-3 sp around, join. *(6 petals)*

Rnd 3: Working behind petals, ch 4, *sc in **back strands** *(see illustration on page 40)* of first sc on next petal, ch 3; repeat from * around, join with sl st in first ch of first ch-4.

Rnd 4: Ch 1, (sc, ch 1, 7 dc, ch 1, sc) in each ch-3 sp around, join with sl st in first sc.

Rnd 5: Working behind petals, ch 5, (sc in back strands of first sc on next petal, ch 4) around, join with sl st in first ch of first ch-5.

Rnd 6: Ch 1, (sc, ch 1, 4 dc, tr, 4 dc, ch 1, sc) in each ch-4 sp around, join with sl st in first sc. Fasten off.

With sewing needle and thread, sew Rose to front of Heart *(see photo).*

For **hanger,** fold ribbon in half; tack ends to back of Heart.

Sew Rose to side of Ornament as shown in photo.

For **hanger,** weave ribbon through two sts of rnd 17, tie ends in a knot.

For **Tassel** *(see illustration below),* cut 85 strands of gold each 8" long. Holding all strands together, tie a separate strand of gold tightly around center of all strands; fold strands in half at center tie. Wrap separate strand of gold around all strands ¼" from top of fold, tie ends securely, leaving long enough ends to hide inside Tassel. Trim ends. ✿

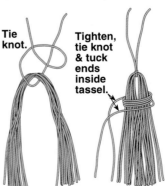

Tie knot.

Tighten, tie knot & tuck ends inside tassel.

continued on page 44

Chenille Ornaments

continued from page 43

Garland

Finished Size: Adjustable to any length desired.

Materials:
- ❑ 50 yds. red chenille sport yarn for each foot of finished Garland
- ❑ 50 yds. gold/gold metallic size 10 crochet cotton thread for each foot of finished Garland
- ❑ No. 0 and No. 5 steel hooks

Gauge: Each Ring is 2" × 2½".

Basic Stitches: Ch, sl st, sc, dc.

First Ring
Rnd 1: With No. 0 hook and red, ch 15, sl st in first ch to form ring, ch 3, 29 dc in ring, join with sl st in top of ch-3. Fasten off. *(First 3 chs count as first dc—30 dc made.)*

Rnd 2: Using No. 5 hook, join gold with sc in any st, ch 2, (sc in next st, ch 2) around, join with sl st in first sc. Fasten off.

Second Ring
Rnd 1: Ch 15; with right side of sts facing you, thread end of ch-15 through First Ring, join with sl st in first ch *(to form Second Ring)*, ch 3, work 29 dc in ring, join with sl st in top of ch-3. Fasten off.

Rnd 2: Using No. 5 hook, join gold with sc in any st, ch 2, (sc in next st, ch 2) around, join with sl st in first sc. Fasten off.

Repeat Second Ring until Garland is desired length. Each new Ring is interlocked with the one before it; always thread the ch-15 through Ring in the same direction. ❋

Bible Cover

continued from page 37

hook, sc in each ch across, turn. *(42 sc made)*

Rows 2–3: Ch 1, sc in each st across, turn. At end of last row, fasten off.

Tie (make 2)
With peach, ch 43, sc in second ch from hook, sc in each ch across. Fasten off.

Assembly
1: For **inside of Cover,** tack one end on one Handle 12 sts from end of row 1 on Cover, skip 6 sts, tack other end of Handle 12 sts from end of same row. Center and tack one end of one Tie to row 1 on Cover between Handle ends. Repeat with other Handle and Tie tacking ends on row 72 of Cover.

2: For **Front,** center and sew rnd 25 of Front Pocket over rows 3–29 on Cover leaving opening unsewn *(see photo).*

3: Center and sew long edges and one short edge on Pencil Pocket over rows 9–20 on one Flap leaving other short edge unsewn for opening. Matching edges, sew Flap to inside Cover on right-hand side leaving inside long edge unsewn for opening.

4: Matching edges, sew other Flap to opposite end of inside Cover leaving one long edge unsewn for opening.

Edging
Rnd 1: With right side of Cover facing you, working through both thicknesses as needed *(do not work over Handles and Ties)*, in sts and in ends of rows, join peach with sc in top right-hand corner on long edge, 2 sc in same corner, evenly space 70 sc across, 3 sc in next corner, evenly space 40 sc across short edge, 3 sc in next corner, evenly space 70 sc across other long edge, 3 sc in next corner, evenly space 40 sc across last short edge, join with sl st in first sc. Fasten off. *(232 sc made)*

Rnd 2: Join white with sc in center st at first corner, 2 sc in same st, sc in each st around with 3 sc in each center st at corner, join. *(240 sc)*

Rnd 3: Ch 1, (sc, ch 3, dc) in first st, skip next 2 sts, *(sc, ch 3, dc) in next st, skip next 2 sts; repeat from * around, join. Fasten off. ❋

Kitchen Quickies

Chapter Three — Fast Food to Feed Your Crochet Frenzy!

The best thing to make for dinner may be reservations, but the best thing that you can make for your kitchen are the anything-but-ordinary creations in this chapter! From place mats to pitcher covers, we've got them all here!

Watermelon Place Mat

Designed by Nanette Seale

Finished Sizes: Place Mat is 12" × 19". Coaster is 5" across. Napkin Ring is 6" around.

Materials:
- ❑ Worsted yarn:
    - 4 oz. pink
    - 2½ oz. green
    - 1½ oz. white
- ❑ 3 yds. black ¼" satin ribbon
- ❑ Black sewing thread and needle
- ❑ Tapestry and sewing needles
- ❑ H hook or hook needed to obtain gauge

Gauge: 7 dc = 2"; 2 dc rows = 1⅛".

Basic Stitches: Ch, sl st, sc, hdc, dc.

Place Mat

Rnd 1: With pink, ch 30, 4 dc in fourth ch from hook, dc in next 25 chs, 5 dc in last ch; working in remaining lps on opposite side of starting ch, dc in next 25 chs, join with sl st in top of ch-3. *(60 dc made)*

Rnd 2: (Ch 3, dc) in first st, 2 dc in each of next 4 sts, dc in next 25 sts, 2 dc in each of next 5 sts, dc in last 25 sts, join. *(70)*

Rnd 3: (Ch 3, dc) in first st, dc in next st, (2 dc in next st, dc in next st) 4 times, dc in next 25 sts, (2 dc in next st, dc in next st) 5 times, dc in each st around, join. *(80)*

Rnd 4: (Ch 3, dc) in first st, dc in each of next 2 sts, (2 dc in next st, dc in each of next 2 sts) 4 times, dc in next 25 sts, (2 dc in next st, dc in each of next 2 sts) 5 times, dc in each st around, join. *(90)*

Rnd 5: (Ch 3, dc) in first st, dc in each of next 3 sts, (2 dc in next st, dc in each of next 3 sts) 4 times, dc in next 25 sts, (2 dc in next st, dc in each of next 3 sts) 5 times, dc in each st around, join. *(100)*

Rnd 6: (Ch 3, dc) in first st, dc in next 4 sts, (2 dc in next st, dc in next 4 sts) 4 times, dc in next 25 sts, (2 dc in next st, dc in next 4 sts) 5 times, dc in each st around, join. *(110)*

Rnd 7: (Ch 3, dc) in first st, dc in next 5 sts, (2 dc in next st, dc in next 5 sts) 4 times, dc in next 25 sts, (2 dc in next st, dc in next 5 sts) 5 times, dc in each st around, join. *(120)*

Rnd 8: (Ch 3, dc) in first st, dc in next 6 sts, (2 dc in next st, dc in next 6 sts) 4 times, dc in next 25 sts, (2 dc in next st, dc in next 6 sts) 5 times, dc in each st around, join. *(130)*

Rnd 9: (Ch 3, dc) in first st, dc in next 7 sts, (2 dc in next st, dc in next 7 sts) 4 times, dc in next 25 sts, (2 dc in next st, dc in next 7 sts) 5 times, dc in each st around, join. Fasten off. *(140)*

Rnd 10: Working in **back lps** *(see Stitch Guide),* join white with sl st in first st, (ch 2, hdc) in same st as sl st, (hdc in each of next 3 sts, 2 hdc in next st) 11 times, hdc in next 25 sts, (2 hdc in next st, hdc in each of next 3 sts) 12 times, hdc in each st around, join with sl st in top of ch-2. Fasten off. *(Ch-2 counts as hdc—164 hdc)*

Rnd 11: Working in **back lps,** join green with sl st in first st, (ch 3, dc) in same st as sl st, (dc in next 5 sts, 2 dc in next st) 10 times, dc in next 21 sts, 2 dc in next st, (dc in next 5 sts, 2 dc in next st) 10 times, dc in last 21 sts, join with sl st in top of ch-3. *(186 dc)*

Rnd 12: Ch 1, reverse sc *(see Stitch Guide)* in each st around, join with sl st in first sc. Fasten off.

Cut one piece each 18", 24" and 30" long from satin ribbon.

Using 18" piece on rnd 1, 24" piece on rnd 3 and 30" piece on rnd 5, weave ribbon pieces through sts of rnds, going over one stitch and under two stitches. With black sewing thread and needle, tack ends of each piece together on wrong side of work.

Coaster

Rnd 1: With pink, for **slip ring** *(see Stitch Guide),* leaving 4" end on yarn, lap yarn over 4" end forming a lp, insert hook through lp from front to back, yo, pull through lp to form ring, yo, pull through lp on hook, ch 3, 14 dc in ring, pull end tightly to close ring, join with sl st in top of ch-3. *(15 dc made)*

Rnd 2: (Ch 3, dc) in first st, 2 dc in each st around, join. *(30)*

Rnd 3: (Ch 3, dc) in first st, dc in next st, (2 dc in next st, dc in next st) around, join. Fasten off. *(45)*

Rnd 4: Working in **back lps,** join white with sc in first st, sc in each st around, join with sl st in first sc. Fasten off.

Rnd 5: Working in **back lps,** join green with sc in first st, sc in next st, 2 sc in next st, (sc in each of next 2 sts, 2 sc in next st) around, join. *(60 sc)*

Rnd 6: Ch 1, reverse sc in each st around, join. Fasten off.

Cut one piece each 8" and 10" long from satin ribbon.

Using 8" on rnd 1 and 10" on rnd 2, weave
continued on page 49

Jar Doilies

An Original by Annie

An Original by Annie ™

Finished Sizes: Small Cover fits 2¼"-diameter jar lid. Medium Cover fits 2¾"-diameter jar lid. Large cover fits 3½"-diameter jar lid.

Materials:
❑ Acrylic sport yarn:
    1 oz. each peach and blue
    ½ oz. ecru
    ½ oz. white *(for optional contrasting color)*
❑ 22" of ¼" or ⅜" desired color ribbon
❑ 12"-square quilt batting
❑ No. 1 steel hook or hook needed to obtain gauge

Gauge: 7 dc = 1", 3 dc rows = 1"; tr is ½" tall.

Basic Stitches: Ch, sl st, sc, hdc, dc, tr.

Lid Cover

Note: Instructions are for Small Cover; changes for Medium and Large Covers are in [ ].

Rnd 1: With main color; make **slip ring** *(see Stitch Guide),* ch 3, 13 dc in ring, pull end tightly to close ring, join with sl st in top of ch-3. *(14 dc made)*

Rnd 2: Ch 1, sc in first st, ch 2 *(counts as first dc),* 2 dc in each st around, dc in same st as sc, join with sl st in top of ch-2. *(28)*

Rnd 3: Ch 1, sc in first st, ch 2, dc in next st, (2 dc in next st, dc in next st) around, dc in same st as sc, join. *(42)*

Rnd 4: Ch 1, sc in first st, ch 2, dc in each of next 2 sts, (2 dc in next st, dc in each of next 2 sts) around, dc in same st as sc, join. *(56)* For **Small only,** using crocheted piece as pattern, cut circle from double thickness of quilt batting.

Rnd [5, 5]: For **Medium and Large only,** ch 1, sc in first st, ch 2, dc in each of next 3 sts, (2 dc in next st, dc in each of next 3 sts) around, dc in same st as sc, join. *[70]* For **Medium only,** using crocheted piece as pattern, cut circle from double thickness of quilt batting.

Rnd [6]: For **Large only,** ch 1, sc in first st, ch 2, dc in next 4 sts, (2 dc in next st, dc in next 4 sts) around, dc in same st as sc, join. *[84]* Using crocheted piece as pattern, cut circle from double thickness of quilt batting.

Rnds 5–6 [6–7, 7–8]: For **all sizes,** ch 1, sc in first st, ch 2, dc in each st around, join.

Rnd 7 [8, 9]: Ch 1, sc in first st, ch 2, dc next 2 sts tog, (dc in next st, dc next 2 sts tog) 15 [21, 27] times, dc in last 8 [4, 0] sts, join. *(40) [48; 56]* For **optional contrasting color edging,** fasten off here and join contrasting color with sl st in first st of this rnd; for **main color edging, do not fasten off.**

Rnd 8 [9, 10]: Ch 5, skip next st, (tr in next st, ch 1, skip next st) around, join with sl st in fourth ch of ch-5. *(20 tr, 20 ch sps) [24 tr, 24 ch sps; 28 tr, 28 ch sps]*

Rnd 9 [10, 11]: Sc in next ch sp, (ch 3, sc in next ch sp) around; for **last ch sp,** ch 1, dc in first sc.

Rnd 10 [11, 12]: Ch 1, 3 sc in last ch sp made, 5 sc in each ch sp around, 2 sc in same ch sp as first 3 sc, join with sl st in first sc.

Rnd 11 [12, 13]: Ch 2, skip next 4 sts, (dc, ch 5, dc) in next st, ch 2, skip next 4 sts, *sc in next st, ch 2, skip next 4 sts, (dc, ch 5, dc) in next st, ch 2, skip next 4 sts; repeat from * around, join with sl st in joining sl st of last rnd.

Rnd 12 [13, 14]: Ch 2, 9 dc in next ch-5 sp, (hdc in next sc, 9 dc in next ch-5 sp) around, join with sl st in top of ch-2. Fasten off.

Finishing

Place batting circle inside Cover.

Weave ribbon through sts of beading rnd. Place Cover on lid. Pull ends of ribbon, gathering Cover to fit around rim of lid. Tie ends in bow. ☞

Watermelon Place Mat

continued from page 47

ribbons in same manner as Place Mat. With black sewing thread and needle, tack ends of each piece together on wrong side of work.

Napin Ring

Rnd 1: With pink, ch 20, sl st in first ch to form ring, ch 1, sc in each ch around, join with sl st in first sc. *(20 sc made)*

Rnd 2: Ch 3, dc in each st around, join with sl st in top of ch-3.

Rnd 3: Ch 1, sc in each st around, join with sl st in first sc. Fasten off.

Rnd 4: Join white with sc in first st, sc in each st around, join. Fasten off.

Rnd 5: Join green with sl st in first st, ch 1, reverse sc in each st around, join. Fasten off.

Rnd 6: Working in remaining lps on opposite side of starting ch on rnd 1, join white with sc in first ch, sc in each ch around, join. Fasten off.

Rnd 7: Join green with sl st in first st, ch 1, reverse sc in each st around, join. Fasten off.

Cut 10" from satin ribbon; weave ribbon through rnd 2 in same manner as Place Mat. With black sewing thread and needle, tack ends together on wrong side of work. ☞

Butterfly Fridgies

Designed by Sandra Evans

Finished Sizes: Small Butterfly is 3" × 3½". Medium Butterfly is 3½" × 5". Large Butterfly is 4½" × 5.

Materials:
- ❑ Small amount each white, green, rose and blue worsted yarn
- ❑ 3 white 6mm chenille stems
- ❑ 3 piece magnetic strip 1" long
- ❑ Craft glue
- ❑ G hook or hook needed to obtain gauge

Gauge: 4 sc = 1"; 4 sc rows = 1".

Basic Stitches: Ch, sl st, sc, dc, tr.

Special Stitches: For **picot**, ch 2, sc in second ch from hook.

For **3-dc popcorn (3-dc pc)**, 3 dc in ch sp, drop lp from hook, insert hook in top of first dc of group, pull dropped lp through st.

For **4-dc popcorn (4-dc pc)**, 4 dc in ch sp, drop lp from hook, insert hook in top of first dc of group, pull dropped lp through st.

For **4-tr popcorn (4-tr pc)**, 4 tr in ch sp, drop lp from hook, insert hook in top of first tr of group, pull dropped lp through st.

Small Butterfly

Rnd 1: With white, ch 8, sl st in first ch to form ring, (ch 3, 2 dc, ch 2) in ring, (3 dc in ring, ch 2) 7 times, join with sl st in top of ch-3. Fasten off. *(24 dc, 8 ch sps made)*

Rnd 2: Join green with sl st in third st of any 3-dc group, *(dc, **picot**—*see Special Stitches*) 4 times in next ch sp, dc in same ch sp as first dc, skip next 2 sts, sl st in next st; repeat from * 6 more times, (dc, picot) 4 times in next ch sp, dc in same ch sp, join with sl st in first sl st. Fasten off.

Finishing

Fold Butterfly in half with wrong sides together. Cut one piece chenille stem 7" long, fold in half. Place last rnd of folded Butterfly in fold of chenille stem. Twist ends of chenille stem together 1" from fold to form wings.

Spread ends of stem apart. Roll each end for antenna.

Glue one magnetic strip centered on back.

Medium Butterfly

Rnd 1: With rose, ch 8, sl st in first ch to form ring, (ch 3, dc, ch 2) in ring, (2 dc in ring, ch 2) 7 times, join with sl st in top of ch-3. Fasten off. *(16 dc, 8 ch sps made)*

Rnd 2: Join white with sl st in any ch sp, ch 3, **3-dc pc** *(see Special Stitches)* in same ch sp as first sl st, ch 4, **4-dc pc** *(see Special Stitches)* in same ch sp, ch 2, (4-dc pc, ch 4, 4-dc pc, ch 2) in each ch sp around, join. Fasten off.

Rnd 3: Join rose with sl st in any ch-2 sp, (2 dc, ch 2, 3-dc pc, ch 2, **4-tr pc**—*see Special Stitches,* ch 2, 3-dc pc, ch 2, 2 dc) in next ch-4 sp, *sl st in next ch-2 sp, (2 dc, ch 2, 3-dc pc, ch 2, 4-tr pc, ch 2, 3-dc pc, ch 2, 2 dc) in next ch-4 sp; repeat from * around, join with sl st in first sl st. Fasten off.

Finishing

With 7½" piece chenille stem, work same as Small Butterfly Finishing.

Large Butterfly

Rnd 1: With blue, ch 8, sl st in first ch to form ring, (ch 3, dc, ch 2) in ring, (2 dc in ring, ch 2) 7 times, join with sl st in top of ch-3. Fasten off. *(16 dc, 8 ch sps made)*

Rnd 2: Join white with sl st in any ch sp, (ch 6, sl st, ch 8, sl st, ch 6, sl st, ch 3) in same ch sp as first sl st, (sl st, ch 6, sl st, ch 8, sl st, ch 6, sl st, ch 3) in each ch sp around, join with sl st in first sl st. Fasten off.

Rnd 3: Join blue with sc in any ch-3 sp, *(dc, picot) 2 times in next ch-6 sp, (tr, picot) 4 times in next ch-8 sp, (dc, picot) 2 times in next ch-6 sp, sc in next ch-3 sp; repeat from * 6 more times, (dc, picot) 2 times in next ch-6 sp, (tr, picot) 4 times in next ch-8 sp, (dc, picot) 2 times in next ch-6 sp, join with sl st in first sc. Fasten off.

Finishing

With 8" piece chenille stem, work same as Small Butterfly Finishing.

Bear Pair Potholder

Designed by Michele Wilcox

Finished Size: 8" tall.

Materials:
- ❑ Worsted yarn:
    - 4 oz. off-white
    - Small amount each black and pink
- ❑ Small amount each black and beige sport yarn
- ❑ Tapestry needle
- ❑ D and F hooks or hooks needed to obtain gauges

Gauges: D hook and sport yarn, 6 sc = 1"; 6 sc rows = 1". **F hook and worsted yarn,** 9 sc = 2"; 5 sc rows = 1".

Basic Stitches: Ch, sl st, sc.

Note: Use F hook and worsted yarn unless otherwise stated.

Big Bear

Side (make 2)
Row 1: With off-white, ch 25, sc in second ch from hook, sc in each ch across, turn. *(24 sc made)*

Row 2: Ch 1, 2 sc in first st, sc in each st across with 2 sc in last st, turn. *(26)*

Rows 3–13: Ch 1, sc in each st across, turn.

Row 14: Ch 1, sc in first st, sc next 2 sts tog, sc in each st across to last 3 sts, sc next 2 sts tog, sc in last st, turn. *(24)*

Rows 15–17: Ch 1, sc in each st across, turn.

Rows 18–29: Repeat rows 14–17 consecutively. At end of last row *(18)*.

Rows 30–35: Repeat row 14. At end of last row, **do not turn.** *(6)*

Rnd 36: Working around outer edge, ch 1, sc in end of each row and in each st around, join with sl st in first sc. Fasten off.

For **front,** with black worsted, using French knot, satin stitch and straight stitch *(see Stitch Guide),* embroider facial features over rows 28–31 on one Side according to photo.

With right side facing you, hold both Side pieces wrong sides together, matching sts; working through both thicknesses in **back lps** *(see Stitch Guide),* join off-white with sl st in center top st, sl st in each st around; for **hanging loop,** ch 12; join with sl st in first sl st. Fasten off.

Ear Piece (make 4)
Row 1: With off-white, ch 4, sc in second ch from hook, sc in each ch across, turn. *(3 sc made)*

Row 2: Ch 1, 2 sc in each st across, turn. *(6)*

Rows 3–4: Ch 1, sc in each st across, turn.

Row 5: Ch 1, sc first 2 sts tog, (sc next 2 sts tog) across, **do not turn.**

Rnd 6: Working around outer edge, ch 1, sc in end of each row and in each st around with 2 sc in each end of row 1 and row 5, join with sl st in first sc. Fasten off.

For **each Ear,** hold two pieces wrong sides together, matching sts; working through both thicknesses in **back lps,** join off-white with sl st in any st, sl st in each st around, join with sl st in first sl st. Fasten off.

Sew to top seam according to photo.

Arm (make 2)
Row 1: With off-white, ch 4, sc in second ch from hook, sc in each ch across, turn. *(3 sc made)*

Row 2: Ch 1, 2 sc in first st, sc in next st, 2 sc in last st, turn. *(5)*

Rows 3–10: Ch 1, sc in each st across, turn.

Row 11: Ch 1, sc first 2 sts tog, sc in next st, sc last 2 sts tog, turn. *(3)*

Row 12: Ch 1, sc 3 sts tog, **do not turn.**

Rnd 13: Working around outer edge, ch 1, sc in end of each row and 3 sc in each st around, join with sl st in first sc. Fasten off.

Paw (make 2)
Row 1: With off-white, ch 6, sc in second ch from hook, sc in each ch across, turn. *(5 sc made)*

Row 2: Ch 1, 2 sc in first st, sc in each st across with 2 sc in last st, turn. *(7)*

Row 8: Ch 1, sc first 2 sts tog, sc in each of next 3 sts, sc last 2 sts tog, **do not turn.** *(5)*

Rnd 9: Working around outer edge, ch 1, sc in end of each row and in each st around with 2 sc in each corner, join with sl st in first sc. Fasten off.

Pad (make 6)
With pink, ch 2, 6 sc in second ch from hook, join with sl st in first sc. Fasten off.

Sew three Pads to each Paw according to photo.

Baby Bear

Body
Row 1: With D hook and beige, ch 13, sc in

continued on page 57

Bessie the Cow

Designed by Michele Wilcox

Finished Size: Approximately 25" tall.

Materials:
- ❑ Worsted yarn:
  - 5 oz. white
  - 3 oz. gray
  - 2 oz. peach
  - 2 oz. black
  - Small amount each green, gold and brown
- ❑ 3½ yds. jute twine
- ❑ 1" × 1¼" cow bell
- ❑ Polyester fiberfill
- ❑ Low-temp glue gun and glue stick
- ❑ Tapestry needle
- ❑ F hook or hook needed to obtain gauge

Gauge: 9 sc = 2"; 9 sc rows = 2".

Basic Stitches: Ch, sl st, sc, hdc, dc.

Note: When **changing colors** (see Stitch Guide), drop first color to wrong side of work, pick up next color. Always change colors in last made.

Body

Row 1: With white, ch 40, sc in second ch from hook, sc in each ch across, turn. (39 sc made)

Row 2: Working in **back lps** (see Stitch Guide), ch 1, sc in each st across changing to gray in last st made (see Note), turn.

Rows 3–4: Working in **back lps**, ch 1, sc in each st across, turn. At end of last row, change to white in last st.

Rows 5–6: Working in **back lps**, ch 1, sc in each st across, turn. At end of last row, change to gray in last st.

Rows 7–72: Repeat rows 3–6 consecutively, ending with row 4. At end of last row, fasten off all colors.

Sew first and last rows together for center front seam. Sew ends of rows on one end together for bottom seam, leaving other end open for top.

Neck Ruffle

Rnd 1: Join gray with sc in end of any row at top opening, skip next row, 5 dc in end of next row, skip next row, (sc in end of next row, skip next row, 5 dc in end of next row, skip next row) around, join with sl st in first sc, **do not turn.** (108 sts made)

Rnd 2: Ch 1, sc in first st, hdc in next st, dc in next st, 3 dc in next st, dc in next st, hdc in next st, (sc in next st, hdc in next st, dc in next st, 3 dc in next st, dc in next st, hdc in next st) around, join. Fasten off. Stuff.

Cut 24" from twine. Starting at center front, lace twine through sts at bottom of Neck Ruffle on rnd 1; pull ends together leaving a 2" diameter opening. Tie ends to cow bell and tie in bow. Trim ends.

Head Side (make 2)

Row 1: With white, ch 13, sc in second ch from hook, sc in each ch across, turn. (12 sc made)

Row 2: Ch 1, 2 sc in first st, sc in each st across to last st, 2 sc in last st, turn. (14)

Row 3: Ch 1, sc in each st across, turn.

Rows 4–9: Repeat rows 2 and 3 alternately. At end of last row (20).

Row 10: Ch 1, sc in each st across, turn.

Rows 11–13: Ch 1, sc first 2 sts tog, sc in each st across to last 2 sts, sc last 2 sts tog, turn. At end of last row (14).

Rows 14–19: Ch 1, sc in each st across, turn.

Rows 20–21: Ch 1, sc first 2 sts tog, sc in each st across to last 2 sts, sc last 2 sts tog, turn.

Rnd 22: Working around outer edge, 2 sc in first st, sc across with 2 sc in last st; working in ends of rows, skip first row, sc in next 11 rows, 2 sc in next row, sc in next 7 rows, skip next row; working in remaining lps on opposite side of starting ch on row 1, 2 sc in first ch, sc across with 2 sc in last ch; working in ends of rows, skip next row, sc in next 7 rows, 2 sc in next row, sc in next 11 rows, skip last row, join with sl st in first sc. Fasten off.

Matching sts, sew Head pieces together in **back lps,** stuffing before closing.

Muzzle

Row 1: With peach, ch 11, sc in second ch from hook, sc in each ch across, turn. (10 sc made)

Rows 2–4: Ch 1, 2 sc in first st, sc in each st across to last st, 2 sc in last st, turn. At end of last row (16).

Rows 5–7: Ch 1, sc in each st across, turn.

Rows 8–10: Ch 1, sc first 2 sts tog, sc in each st across to last 2 sts, sc last 2 sts tog, turn. At end of last row (10).

Rnd 11: Working around outer edge, ch 1, sc in each st and in end of each row around, join with sl st in first sc. **Do not turn.**

Rnd 12: Ch 1, sc in each st around, join. Fasten off.

continued on page 56

Bessie the Cow

continued from page 55

Stuff. Sew last rnd of Muzzle centered over rows 4–13 on one side of Head for front.

For **nostrils,** with tapestry needle and peach, make two tiny tacking sts on rnd 7 of Muzzle centered 1½" apart, pulling tightly to form indention.

With tapestry needle and black, embroider satin stitches *(see Stitch Guide)* over rows 14–16 of Head centered 1¼" apart for eyes; embroider straight stitches and fly stitch *(see Stitch Guide)* centered over rows 2–5 of Muzzle *(see facial feature illustration)* for mouth.

Ear Back (make 2)
Row 1: With white, ch 7, sc in second ch from hook, sc in each ch across, turn. *(6 sc made)*
Row 2: Ch 1, 2 sc in first st, sc in each st across to last st, 2 sc in last st, turn. *(8)*
Row 3: Ch 1, sc in each st across, turn.
Rows 4–5: Ch 1, 2 sc in first st, sc in each st across to last st, 2 sc in last st, turn. *(10, 12)*
Rows 6–9: Ch 1, sc in each st across, turn.
Rows 10–13: Ch 1, sc first 2 sts tog, sc in each st across to last 2 sts, sc last 2 sts tog, turn. At end of last row *(4).*
Rnd 14: Working around outer edge, ch 1, sc in each st and in end of each row around, join with sl st in first sc. Fasten off.

Ear Front (make 2)
Rows 1–13: With peach, repeat rows 1–13 of Ear Back. At end of last row, **do not turn.** Fasten off.
Rnd 14: Working around outer edge, join white with sc in first st, sc in each st and in end of each row and in remaining lps on opposite side of starting ch around, join with sl st in first sc. Fasten off.
Matching sts, working in **back lps,** sew one Ear Front and one Ear Back together. Fold row 1 in half, sew together. Repeat with remaining Ear pieces.
Sew Ears to top of Head 3" apart.

Horn (make 2)
Note: Work in continuous rnds; do not join or turn unless otherwise stated. Mark first st of each rnd.
Rnd 1: With gray, ch 2, 6 sc in second ch from hook. *(6 sc made)*
Rnd 2: (2 sc in next st, sc in next st) around. *(9)*
Rnds 3–8: Sc in each st around. At end of last rnd, join with sl st in first sc. Fasten off. Stuff. Sew Horns 1" apart to top of Head between Ears. Glue bottom of Head to inside of Neck Ruffle.

Spot (make 5)
Rnd 1: With black, ch 2, 6 sc in second ch from hook, **do not join.** *(6 sc made)*
Rnd 2: 2 sc in each st around. *(12)*
Rnd 3: (Sc, ch 1, dc) in next st, (dc, ch 1, sc) in next st, *(sc, ch 1, dc) in next st, 2 dc in next st, (dc, ch 1, sc) in next st; repeat from * 2 more times, skip last st, join with sl st in first sc. Fasten off. Set aside to be used later.

Arm Side (make 4)
Row 1: Starting at bottom, with black, ch 7, sc in second ch from hook, sc in each ch across, turn. *(6 sc made)*
Row 2: Ch 1, 2 sc in first st, sc in each st across to last st, 2 sc in last st, turn. *(8)*
Rows 3–5: Ch 1, sc in each st across, turn. At end of last row, change to white in last st made. Fasten off black.
Rows 6–19: Ch 1, sc in each st across, turn.
Row 20: Ch 1, sc first 2 sts tog, sc in each st across to last 2 sts, sc last 2 sts tog, **do not turn.**
Rnd 21: Working around outer edge, ch 1, sc in end of row and in each st around changing colors as needed to match piece, join with sl st in first sc. Fasten off.
For **Arm** *(make 2),* matching sts and colors, sew two Arm Side pieces together through **back lps**.
Using black, sew one Spot to one side of each Arm.
Cut two pieces each 15" long from twine. Tie one 15" piece to top of each Arm. Tie Arms to each side of Body directly below Ears. Trim ends.

Thigh Side (make 4)
Row 1: With white, ch 9, sc in second ch from hook, sc in each ch across, turn. *(8 sc made)*
Row 2: Ch 1, 2 sc in first st, sc in each st across to last st, 2 sc in last st, turn. *(10)*
Rows 3–13: Ch 1, sc in each st across, turn.
Row 14: Ch 1, sc first 2 sts tog, sc in each st across to last 2 sts, sc last 2 sts tog, **do not turn.**
Rnd 15: Working around outer edge, ch 1, sc in end of each row and in each st around, join with sl st in first sc. Fasten off.
For **Thigh** *(make 2),* matching sts, sew two Thigh Side pieces together through **back lps.**
Using black, sew one Spot to one side of one Thigh.
Cut two pieces each 15" long from twine. Tie one 15" piece to top of each Thigh. Tie Thighs to center bottom of Body 3" apart. Trim ends.

Calf Side (make 4)
Row 1: Starting at bottom, with black, ch 9, sc in second ch from hook, sc in each ch across, turn. *(8 sc made)*
Row 2: Ch 1, 2 sc in first st, sc in each st across to last st, 2 sc in last st, turn. *(10)*
Rows 3–5: Ch 1, sc in each st across, turn. At end of last row, change to white in last st made.
Rows 6–12: Ch 1, sc in each st across, turn.
Row 13: Ch 1, sc first 2 sts tog, sc in each st across to last 2 sts, sc last 2 sts tog, turn. *(8)*
Rows 14–20: Ch 1, sc in each st across, turn.

Rnd 21: Working around outer edge, ch 1, sc in end of each row and in each st around changing colors as needed to match piece, join with sl st in first sc. Fasten off all colors.

For **Calf** *(make 2),* matching sts and colors, sew two Calf Side pieces together through **back lps**.

Using black, sew one Spot to one side of each Calf.

Cut two pieces each 15" long from twine. Tie one 15" piece to bottom of each Calf. Trim ends.

Sunflower

Rnd 1: With brown, ch 2, 6 sc in second ch from hook, **do not join.** *(6 sc made)*

Rnd 2: 2 sc in each st around changing to gold in last st made. *(12)*

Rnd 3: (Ch 3, sl st in next sc) around, ch 3, join with sl st in first ch of first ch-3. Fasten off.

Leaf (make 2)

With green, ch 6, sc in second ch from hook, hdc in next ch, dc in each of next 2 chs, 6 dc in last ch; working in remaining lps on opposite side of ch-6, dc in each of next 2 chs, hdc in next ch, sc in next ch, join with sl st in first sc. Fasten off.

Using matching colors, sew Leaves and Flower to top of Head beside one Ear. 🖙

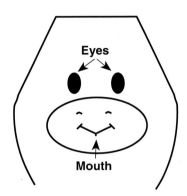

Bear Pair Potholder

continued from page 53

second ch from hook, sc in each ch across, turn. *(12 sc made)*

Rows 2–7: Repeat rows 2–7 of Big Bear's Side. *(14)*

Row 8: Ch 1, sc in first st, sc next 2 sts tog, sc in each st across to last 3 sts, sc next 2 sts tog, sc in last st, turn. *(12)*

Rows 9–10: Ch 1, sc in each st across, turn.

Row 11: Repeat row 8. *(10)*

Rows 12–13: Ch 1, sc in each st across, turn.

Rows 14–15: Repeat row 8. *(8, 6)*

Row 16: Ch 1, sc in first st, (sc next 2 sts tog) 2 times, sc in last st, **do not turn.**

Rnd 17: Working around outer edge, ch 1, sc in end of each row and in each st around, join with sl st in first sc. Fasten off.

With black sport yarn, using French knot, straight stitch and satin stitch, embroider facial features over rows 13–15 according to photo.

Sew centered ½" below Big Bear's mouth.

Arm (make 2)

Row 1: With D hook and beige, ch 2, 3 sc in second ch from hook, turn. *(3 sc made)*

Rows 2–6: Ch 1, sc in each st across, turn.

Row 7: Ch 1, sc 3 sts tog, **do not turn.** *(1)*

Rnd 8: Working around outer edge, ch 1, sc in end of each row and 3 sc in each st around, join with sl st in first sc. Fasten off.

Paw (make 2)

Row 1: With D hook and beige, ch 2, 3 sc in second ch from hook, turn. *(3 sc made)*

Row 2: Ch 1, sc in first st, 2 sc in next st, sc in last st, turn. *(4)*

Rows 3–4: Ch 1, sc in each st across, turn.

Row 5: Ch 1, sc in first st, sc next 2 sts tog, sc in last st, turn. *(3)*

Row 6: Ch 1, sc 3 sts tog, **do not turn.** *(1)*

Rnd 7: Working around outer edge, ch 1, sc in end of each row and 3 sc in each st around, join with sl st in first sc. Fasten off.

Ear (make 2)

Rnd 1: With D hook and beige, ch 2, 6 sc in second ch from hook, **do not join.** *(6 sc made)*

Rnd 2: (Sc in next st, 2 sc in next st) around, join with sl st in first sc. Fasten off.

Finishing

Sew remaining pieces on front of Big Bear according to photo. 🖙

Country Potholders

Designed by Ann Parnell

Cross & Crown

Finished Size: 7" square.

Materials:
- ❑ Cotton sport yarn:
    - 2 oz. green
    - 1 oz. each yellow and peach
- ❑ D and E hooks or hook needed to obtain gauge

Gauge: **D and E hooks,** 5 sc = 1"; 5 sc rows = 1".

Basic Stitches: Ch, sl st, sc, hdc.

Special Stitch: For **tapestry sc** *(to be worked on wrong side of work only),* with hook above and behind yarn, insert hook from back to front in top of st, yo, pull through st, yo, pull through both lps on hook.

Notes: When **changing colors** *(see Stitch Guide),* drop first color to wrong side of work, carry and work over dropped color along back, pick up when needed. Always change colors in last st made.
Each square on graph equals one tapestry sc.
When working with tapestry sc and color change, it will cause the stitch to pull down slightly; you will need to use the larger hook to maintain the gauge.

Front
Row 1: With E hook and green, ch 38, sc in second ch from hook, sc in next 10 chs changing to peach in last ch made *(see illustration),* sc in next ch changing to green, sc in next 13 chs changing to peach in last ch made, sc in next ch changing to green, sc in last 11 chs, turn. *(Front of row 1 is right side of work—37 sts made.)*
Row 2: Ch 1, work **tapestry sc** *(see Special Stitch)* in each st across following graph on page 63 for color changes *(see Notes),* turn. *Front of row 2 is wrong side of work.*
Rows 3–37: Ch 1, work sc on odd rows and tapestry sc on all even rows across according to graph, turn. At end of last row, fasten off.

Back
Row 1: With D hook and green, ch 38, sc in second ch from hook, sc in each ch across, turn. *(37 sc made)*
Rows 2–37: Ch 1, sc in each st across, turn.
Rnd 38: For **edging,** hold wrong sides of Front and Back pieces together; working through both thicknesses, ch 1, hdc in each st across; for **hanger,** ch 12; hdc in end of each row and in each st around with 3 hdc in each corner st around, join with sl st in top of ch-1. Fasten off.

Goose Tracks

Finished Size: 7" square.

Materials:
- ❑ Cotton sport yarn:
    - 2 oz. rose
    - 1 oz. each aqua and off-white
- ❑ D and E hooks or hook needed to obtain gauge

Gauge: **D and E hooks,** 5 sc = 1"; 5 sc rows = 1".

Basic Stitches: Ch, sl st, sc, hdc.

Front
Row 1: With E hook and rose, ch 38, sc in second ch from hook, sc in next 4 chs changing to aqua in last ch made *(see illustration on row a of Cross & Crown Front),* sc in next ch changing to rose, sc in next 9 chs changing to aqua in last ch made, sc in next ch changing to off-white, sc in next 5 chs changing to aqua in last ch made, sc in next ch changing to rose, sc in next 9 chs changing to aqua in last ch made, sc in next ch changing to rose, sc in last 5 chs, turn. *(Front of row 1 is right side of work—37 sc made.)*
Row 2: Ch 1, **tapestry sc** *(see Special Stitch on Cross & Crown)* in each st across, following graph on page 63 for color changes *(see Notes on Cross & Crown),* turn. *Front of row 2 is wrong side of work.*
Rows 3–37: Ch 1, work sc on odd rows and tapestry sc on all even rows across according to graph, turn. At end of last row, fasten off.

Back
Row 1: With D hook and rose, ch 38, sc in second ch from hook, sc in each ch across, turn. *(37 sc made)*

continued on page 63

Rag Dining Decor

An Original by Annie

Instructions on page 62

An Original by Annie ™

Rag Dining Decor

photo on pages 60-61

Read Before Starting:

To make strips, tear or cut along the longest measurement of a fabric piece.

To maintain a consistent color as you are crocheting strips from fabric that has a noticeable difference between the right and wrong side, iron them in half lengthwise with wrong sides together before hand so the same side of the fabric is always showing as you work.

Keep a threaded sewing needle handy as you work; when you reach the end of a strip, add a new one by holding the ends right sides together, then sew a ¼" seam using a small running stitch *(see illustration).*

Place Mat

Finished Size: 16½" across.

Materials:
- ❏ Fabric:
    - 57 yds. of 2½"-wide strips *(equivalent to 3¼ yds. of 45"-wide fabric)* Contrasting Color (CC)
    - 21 yds. of 2½"-wide strips *(equivalent to 2¼ yds. of 45"-wide fabric)* Main Color (MC)
- ❏ Sewing thread to match fabric
- ❏ Sewing needle
- ❏ Q bulky hook.

Gauge: 3 sc = 2"; 4 sc rows = 3½".

Basic Stitches: Ch, sl st, sc.

Note: Do not join rnds unless otherwise stated. Mark first st of each rnd.

Place Mat
Rnd 1: With MC, ch 2, 7 sc in second ch from hook *(7 sc made)*

Rnd 2: 2 sc in each st around. *(14 sc)*

Rnd 3: (Sc in next st, 2 sc in next st) around, join with sl st in first sc. Fasten off. *(21)*

Rnd 4: Working this rnd in **back lps** *(see Stitch Guide),* join CC with sc in next st, sc in next st, 2 sc in next st, (sc in each of next 2 sts, 2 sc in next st) around, join with sl st in first sc. *(28) To make the rnds appear continuous, do not work in the first st that has been joined into with a sl st; work in the joining sl st of the previous rnd.*

Rnd 5: Ch 1, (sc in each of next 3 sts, 2 sc in next st) around, skip ch-1, join. Fasten off. *(35)*

Rnd 6: Working this rnd in **back lps,** join MC with sc in next st, sc in each of next 3 sts, 2 sc

in next st, (sc in next 4 sts, 2 sc in next st) around, join. Fasten off. *(42)*

Rnd 7: Working this rnd in **back lps,** join CC with sc in next st, sc in next 4 sts, 2 sc in next st, (sc in next 5 sts, 2 sc in next st) around, join. *(49)*

Rnd 8: Ch 1, sc in first 6 sts, 2 sc in next st, (sc in next 6 sts, 2 sc in next st) around, skip ch-1, join. *(55)*

Rnd 9: Working this rnd in **back lps,** ch 1, sl st in next st and in each st around, skip ch-1, join with sl st in first sl st. Fasten off.

Basket

Finished Size: 10" across.

Materials:
- ❏ Fabric:
    - 50 yds. of 2½"-wide strips *(equivalent to 3 yds. of 45"-wide fabric)* Main Color (MC)
    - 28 yds. of 2½"-wide strips *(equivalent to 1½ yds. of 45"-wide fabric)* Contrasting Color (CC)
- ❏ Sewing thread to match fabric
- ❏ Sewing needle
- ❏ Size Q bulky hook.

Gauge: 3 sc = 2"; 4 sc rows = 3½".

Basic Stitches: Ch, sl st, sc, hdc.

Note: Do not join rnds unless otherwise stated. Mark first st of each rnd.

Basket
Rnd 1: With MC, ch 2, 7 sc in second ch from hook. *(7 sc made)*

Rnd 2: 2 sc in each st around. *(14)*

Rnd 3: (Sc in next st, 2 sc in next st) around. *(21)*

Rnd 4: (Sc in each of next 2 sts, 2 sc in next st) around. *(28)*

Rnd 5: (Sc in each of next 3 sts, 2 sc in next st) around, join with sl st in first sc. Fasten off. *(35)*

Rnd 6: Working this rnd in **back lps** *(see Stitch Guide),* join CC with sc in next st on last rnd, ch 1, hdc in each st around with 2 hdc in joining sl st of last rnd, join with sl st in **back lp** of ch-1. *(36 hdc)*

Rnd 7: Ch 1 loosely, hdc in next st and in each st around, hdc in same st as ch-1, join with sl st in top of first hdc. Fasten off.

Rnd 8: Join MC with sc in next st *(do not work in first st),* sc in each st around, sc in joining sl st of last rnd, join with sl st in first sc. *(36 sc)*

Rnd 9: Working this rnd in **back lps,** ch 1 *(do not work in first st),* sl st in each st around, sl st in joining sl st of last rnd, join with sl st in first sl st. Fasten off.

continued from page 59

Rows 2–37: Ch 1, sc in each st across, turn.

Rnd 38: For **edging,** hold wrong sides of Front and Back pieces together, ch 1, hdc in each st across; for **hanger,** ch 12; (hdc in end of each row or in each st along next side, 3 hdc in corner st) around, join with sl st in top of ch-1. Fasten off. ☞

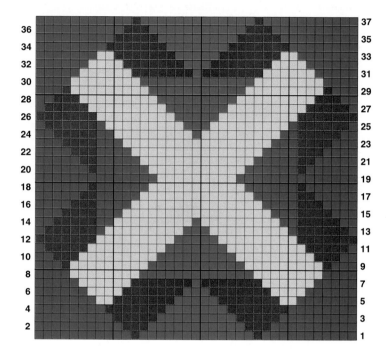

Cross & Crown

■ = Green
▢ = Yellow
■ = Peach

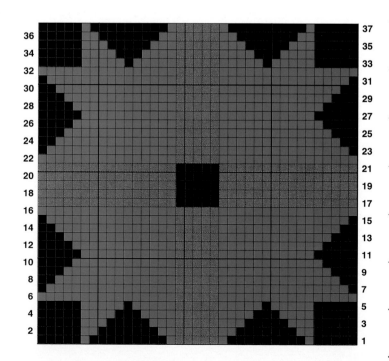

Goose Tracks

■ = Rose
■ = Aqua
▨ = Off-white

Pitcher Covers

Designed by Dot Drake

Finished Sizes: Small Cover is 6" across. Large Cover is 9" across.

Materials:
- ❑ 100 yds. each peach and white size 10 crochet cotton thread
- ❑ Crystal 8mm faceted beads:
  - 17 for Small Cover
  - 33 for Large Cover
- ❑ Craft glue
- ❑ Embroidery needle
- ❑ No. 8 steel hook or hook needed to obtain gauge

Gauge: Rnds 1–7 = 2" across.

Basic Stitches: Ch, sl st, sc, hdc, dc, tr.

Small Cover

Rnd 1: With peach, ch 8, sl st in first ch to form ring, 16 sc in ring, join with sl st in first sc. *(16 sc made)*

Rnd 2: Ch 6, skip next st, (dc in next st, ch 3, skip next st) around, join with sl st in third ch of ch-6. *(8 ch sps)*

Rnd 3: For **petals**, skipping each dc, (sc, hdc, 3 dc, hdc, sc) in each ch sp around, join with sl st in same place as joining sl st on rnd 2. *(8 petals)*

Rnd 4: Working behind petals into skipped dc of rnd 2, ch 7, skip next dc, *sc in **back lp** (see Stitch Guide) of next dc, ch 7, skip next dc; repeat from * around, **do not join.** *(4 ch sps)*

Rnd 5: For **petals**, (sc, hdc, dc, 4 tr, dc, 4 tr, dc, hdc, sc) in each ch sp around. *(4 petals)*

Rnd 6: Working behind petals into ch-7 sps on rnd 4 between center dc and next tr, ch 4, sc behind next petal, (ch 7, sc behind next petal) 3 times, ch 4. *(2 ch-4 sps, 3 ch-7 sps)*

Rnd 7: For **petals**, (sl st, ch 3, 5 tr, dc, hdc, sc) in first ch-4 sp *(this forms half of first petal)*, *(sc, hdc, dc, 5 tr, dc, 5 tr, dc, hdc, sc) in next ch-7 sp; repeat from * 2 more times, (sc, hdc, dc, 5 tr) in last ch-4 sp *(this completes first petal)*, join with sl st in top of ch-3. Fasten off. *(4 petals)*

Rnd 8: Join white with sl st in first tr past any sc, ch 7, skip next 2 sts, sc in next st, ch 7, skip next 3 sts, sc in next st, ch 7, skip next 2 sts, sc in next st, (ch 7, sc in first tr on next petal, ch 7, skip next 2 sts, sc in next st, ch 7, skip next 3 sts, sc in next st, ch 7, skip next 2 sts, sc in next st) around, ch 3, join with dc in first ch of first ch-7. *(6 ch sps)*

Rnds 9–11: Ch 1, (sc, ch 3, sc) in ch-3 sp, *ch 7, (sc, ch 3, sc) in next ch sp; repeat from * around, ch 3, join with dc in first sc. At end of last rnd, fasten off.

Note: With embroidery needle, thread 16 beads onto peach crochet cotton.

Rnd 12: Join peach with sl st in any ch-7 sp, ch 3, (4 dc, ch 1, pull up one bead and ch around bead, ch 1, 5 dc) in same ch sp as joining, (5 dc, ch 1, pull up one bead and ch around bead, ch 1, 5 dc) in each ch sp around, join with sl st in top of ch-3. Fasten off.

Glue remaining bead to center of rnd 1.

Large Cover

Rnds 1–10: Work rnds 1–10 of Small Cover.

Rnd 11: Ch 1, (sc, ch 3, sc) in ch-3 sp, *ch 7, (sc, ch 3, sc) in next ch sp; repeat from * around, ch 7, join with sl st in first sc.

Rnd 12: Sl st in each of next 2 chs, (sc, ch 7, sc) in same ch sp, (ch 7, sc, ch 7, sc) in each ch sp around, ch 3, join with dc in first sc.

Rnds 13–15: Ch 1, (sc, ch 3, sc) in ch-3 sp, *ch 7, (sc, ch 3, sc) in next ch sp; repeat from * around, ch 3, join. At end of last rnd, fasten off.

Note: With embroidery needle, thread 32 beads onto peach crochet cotton thread.

Rnd 16: Work rnd 12 of Small Cover.

Glue remaining bead to center of rnd 1. ☞

Broom Handle Duster

Designed by De-De Albert

Finished Size: 14" long.

Materials:
- ❏ 3 oz. rug yarn
- ❏ J hook

Basic Stitches: Ch, sl st, sc, dc.

Duster

Rnd 1: Ch 4, sl st in first ch to form ring, ch 1, 2 **lp st** *(see illustration below)* in each ch around, join with sl st in first st. *(8 lp sts made)*

Rnd 2: Ch 1, 2 lp st in each st around, join. *(16)* Turn lps to outside of work.

Rnds 3–29: Ch 1, lp st in each st around, join.

Note: To **lp st next 2 sts tog**, *lp st in first st keeping last lps on hook, lp st in next st keeping last lps on hook, yo, pull through all lps on hook.*

Rnd 30: Ch 1, (lp st in each of next 2 sts, lp st next 2 sts tog) around, join. *(12)*

Rnd 31: Ch 1, (lp st in next 4 sts, lp st next 2 sts tog) around, join. *(10)*

Rnd 32: Ch 1, sc in each st around, join with sl st in first sc.

Rnd 33: Ch 3, dc in each st around, join with sl st in top of ch-3.

Rnds 34–36: Repeat rnds 32 and 33 alternately, ending with rnd 32. At end of last rnd, fasten off. ☞

Loop Stitch (lp st): Insert hook in next st, wrap yarn 2 times around 2 fingers, insert hook from left to right through all loops on fingers, pull loops through st, drop loops from fingers, yo, pull through all loops on hook.

Around the House

Chapter Four — Home Accents That Are a Decorator's Delight!

Do you have a spot in your home that begs to be brightened? In the blink of an eye, you can crochet a project that fills the bill perfectly! Inside you'll find projects from luscious and lacy to cute and country!

Victorian Wreath

Designed by Lucille Britain

Finished Size: 23½" across.

Materials:
- ❏ 400 yds. white size 10 crochet cotton thread
- ❏ 15 yds. of 1⅜" ribbon
- ❏ 14" Styrofoam® wreath
- ❏ Bunch of dried baby's breath flowers
- ❏ Assorted silk flowers
- ❏ Craft glue
- ❏ Fabric stiffener
- ❏ One package sequin pins
- ❏ No. 6 steel hook or hook needed to obtain gauge

Gauge: 1 shell = ½"; 5 shell rows = 2".

Basic Stitches: Ch, sl st, sc, dc, tr.

Special Stitches: For **beginning shell (beg shell),** sl st in next st, (sl st, ch 3, dc, ch 1, 2 dc) in next ch sp.
For **shell,** (2 dc, ch 1, 2 dc) in ch sp of next shell.

Doily

Rnd 1: Ch 192, sl st in first ch to form ring, ch 3, dc in next ch, ch 4, skip next 4 chs, (dc in each of next 2 chs, ch 4, skip next 4 chs) around, join with sl st in top of ch-3. *(64 dc, 32 ch sps made)*

Rnd 2: Ch 3, dc in next st, ch 6, skip next ch sp, (dc in each of next 2 sts, ch 6, skip next ch sp) around, join.

Rnd 3: Beg shell *(see Special Stitches),* ch 3, skip next 2 sts, ***shell** *(see Special Stitches)* in next ch sp, ch 3, skip next 2 sts; repeat from * around, join. *(32 shells)*

Rnd 4: Beg shell, ch 4, (shell in next shell, ch 4) around, join.

Rnd 5: Beg shell, ch 5, (shell in next shell, ch 5) around, join.

Rnd 6: Beg shell, ch 6, (shell in next shell, ch 6) around, join.

Rnd 7: Beg shell, ch 7, (shell in next shell, ch 7) around, join.

Rnd 8: Beg shell, ch 7, (2 dc, ch 3, 2 dc) in next shell, ch 7, *shell in next shell, ch 7, (2 dc, ch 3, 2 dc) in next shell, ch 7; repeat from * around, join.

Rnd 9: Beg shell, ch 5, 9 tr in next ch-3 sp, ch 5, (shell in next shell, ch 5, 9 tr in next ch-3 sp, ch 5) around, join.

Rnd 10: Beg shell, *[ch 3, tr in next tr, (ch 1, tr in next tr) 8 times, ch 3], shell in next shell; repeat from * 14 more times; repeat betwen [ ], join.

Rnd 11: Beg shell, *[ch 3, skip next ch sp, sc in next ch-1 sp, (ch 3, sc in next ch sp) 7 times, ch 3, skip next ch sp], shell in next shell; repeat from * 14 more times; repeat between [ ], join.

Rnd 12: Beg shell, *[ch 4, skip next ch sp, sc in next ch sp, (ch 3, sc in next ch sp) 6 times, ch 4, skip next ch sp], shell in next shell; repeat from * 14 more times; repeat between [ ], join.

continued on page 71

Scallop Edge Doily

Designed by Elsie Caddy

Finished Size: 12" across.

Materials:
- ❏ 200 yds. white size 10 crochet cotton thread
- ❏ No. 7 steel hook or hook needed to obtain gauge

Gauge: Rnds 1–4 = 2¼" across.

Basic Stitches: Ch, sl st, sc, dc, tr.

Doily

Rnd 1: Ch 6, sl st in first ch to form ring, ch 3, 23 dc in ring, join with sl st in top of ch-3. *(24 dc made)*

Rnd 2: Ch 4, (dc in next st, ch 1) around, join with sl st in third ch of ch-4. *(24 dc)*

Rnd 3: Sl st in first ch-1 sp, ch 5, (dc in next ch sp, ch 2) around, join with sl st in third ch of ch-5.

Rnd 4: (Ch 3, dc) in first st, ch 2, (2 dc in next st, ch 2) around, join with sl st in top of ch-3.

Rnds 5–6: Sl st across sts into first ch-2 sp, (sc, ch 3, 2 dc) in same ch sp, ch 2, (3 dc in next ch-2 sp, ch 2) around, join.

Rnd 7: Sl st across sts into first ch-2 sp, sc in same ch sp, (ch 6, sc in next ch-2 sp) around to last ch-2 sp, ch 3, dc in last sc.

Rnd 8: (Ch 3, sc) in first ch sp, *ch 6; for **picot, (sc, ch 3, sc)** in next ch sp; repeat from * around, ch 3, dc in top of last ch-3 on last rnd.

Rnds 9–10: (Ch 3, sc) in first ch sp, (ch 7, picot in next ch sp) around, ch 3, tr in top of last ch-3 on last rnd.

Rnd 11: (Ch 3, sc) in first ch sp, (ch 8, picot in next ch sp) around, ch 4, tr in top of last ch-3 on last rnd.

Rnds 12–14: (Ch 3, sc) in first ch sp, (ch 8, picot in next ch sp) around, ch 4, tr in top of last ch-4 on last rnd.

Rnd 15: Sl st in picot, ch 4, dc in same sp, *[ch 6; for **4-dc shell, (2 dc, ch 2, 2 dc)** in next picot; ch 6]; for **V st, (dc, ch 1, dc)** in next picot; repeat from * 10 more times; repeat between [ ], join with sl st in third ch of ch-4.

Rnds 16–17: Sl st in next ch sp, ch 4, dc in same ch sp, *[ch 6; for **6-dc shell, (3 dc, ch 3, 3 dc)** in shell; ch 6]; V st in V st; repeat from * 10 more times; repeat between [ ], join.

Rnds 18–19: Sl st in ch sp, ch 4, dc in same sp, *[ch 6; for **8-dc shell, (4 dc, ch 3, 4 dc)** in shell; ch 6], V st in V st; repeat from * 10 more times; repeat between [ ], join.

Rnd 20: Sl st in next ch sp, ch 4, dc in same sp, *[ch 4, 11 tr in shell, ch 4], V st in V st; repeat from * 10 more times; repeat between [ ], join.

Rnd 21: Sl st in next ch sp, ch 4, dc in same sp, *[ch 2, (tr in next tr, ch 2) 11 times], V st in V st; repeat from * 10 more times; repeat between [ ], join.

Rnd 22: Sl st in next ch sp, sc in same sp, *[ch 2, tr in next tr, (2 tr in next ch sp) 10 times, tr in next tr, ch 2], sc in V st; repeat from * 10 more times; repeat between [ ], join with sl st in first sc.

Rnd 23: Sl st in first 2 chs, *sc in tr, (ch 4, skip 2 tr, sc in sp between tr) 9 times, ch 4, skip 2 tr, sc in next tr, ch 4; repeat from * 11 more times, join with sl st in first sc. Fasten off. 🏠

Rnd 13: Sl st in next st, (sl st, ch 3, dc, ch 2, 2 dc, ch 2, 2 dc) in next ch sp, *[ch 3, skip next ch sp, sc in next ch sp, (ch 3, sc in next ch sp) 5 times, ch 3, skip next ch sp], (2 dc, ch 2, 2 dc, ch 2, 2 dc) in next shell; repeat from * 14 more times; repeat between [ ], join.

Row 14: For **first point,** sl st in next st, sl st in next ch sp, sl st in next st, beg shell, ch 4, skip next ch sp, sc in next ch sp, (ch 3, sc in next ch sp) 4 times, ch 4, skip next ch sp, shell in next ch-2 sp leaving remaining sts unworked, **turn.**

Row 15: Beg shell, ch 4, skip next ch sp, sc in next ch sp, (ch 3, sc in next ch sp) 3 times, ch 4, skip nex ch sp, shell in last shell, turn.

Row 16: Beg shell, ch 3, skip next ch sp, sc in next ch sp, (ch 3, sc in next ch sp) 2 times, ch 3, skip next ch sp, shell in last shell, turn.

Row 17: Beg shell, ch 2, skip next ch sp, sc in next ch sp, ch 3, sc in next ch sp, ch 2, skip next ch sp, shell in last shell, turn.

Row 18: Beg shell, ch 3, skip next ch sp, sc in next ch sp, ch 3, skip next ch sp, shell in last shell, turn, ch 3, sl st in first st of beg shell. Fasten off.

Row 14: For **second point,** join with sl st in next ch-2 sp on rnd 13, (ch 3, dc, ch 1, 2 dc) in same ch sp, ch 4, skip next ch sp, sc in next ch sp, (ch 3, sc in next ch sp) 4 times, ch 4, skip next ch sp, shell in next ch-2 sp, turn.

Rows 15–18: Repeat rows 15–18 of first point.

For **remaining points,** repeat second point 14 more times.

Edging

Rnd 1: Working around outer edge in ends of rows, join with sl st in end of row 14 on any point, (ch 3, dc, ch 1, 2 dc) in same row, *(ch 3, skip next row, shell in next row) 2 times, [ch 2, shell in next ch-3 sp at tip of point, ch 2, shell in next row, (ch 3, skip next row, shell in next row) 2 times, ch 1, skip next 2 sts], shell in next row on next point, (ch 3, skip next row, shell in next row) 2 times; repeat from * 14 more times; repeat between [ ], join with sl st in top of ch-3.

Rnd 2: Sl st back into last ch-1 sp, ch 9, sc in sixth ch from hook, dc in same ch sp, *[ch 3, skip next shell, (sc in next ch sp, ch 3, dc in next shell; for **picot, ch 6, sc in same dc;** dc in same ch sp, ch 3) 5 times, sc in next ch sp, ch 3, skip next shell], (dc, picot, dc) in next ch-1 sp; repeat from * 14 more times; repeat between [ ], join. Fasten off.

Finishing

1: Apply fabric stiffener to Doily. Shape. Let dry.

2: Wrap foam wreath with ribbon, securing with sequin pins on back side until completely covered. Glue ends in place.

3: Glue Doily centered over wreath.

4: Arrange baby's breath and flowers at top of wreath as desired; glue in place. Make a bow of remaining ribbon and glue to center top of wreath over flowers. 🏠

Dream Catchers

Designed by Clare Stringer

Heart's Desire

Finished Size: 3¼" long excluding hanging loop and decoration.

Materials:
- ❏ 1 small spool each of white and blue sewing thread
- ❏ One 2½" and three 1½" bird feathers
- ❏ Beads:
  - 3 clear seed beads
  - Two 5 × 14mm blue and white glass beads
  - 19 small *(3 to 5mm)* beads in assorted colors and shapes
- ❏ One 7mm white heart-shaped bead or button
- ❏ 3" plastic lid *(from yogurt container)*
- ❏ Craft glue
- ❏ Beading needle
- ❏ No. 10 steel hook or hook needed to obtain gauge

Gauge: With 2 strands of thread held together, 10 sts or chs = 1"; rnds 1–2 are ¾" across.

Basic Stitches: Ch, sl st, sc, hdc, dc, tr.

Catcher
Note: *Being careful not to cut into outer rim, remove the entire center from plastic lid leaving outer rim for Frame.*

Rnd 1: Holding white and blue thread together as one, ch 7, sl st in first ch to form ring, ch 1, 12 sc in ring, join with sl st in first sc. *(12 sc made)*

Rnd 2: Ch 1, sc in first st, (ch 5, sc in next st) around, ch 2, join with dc in first sc. *(joining ch sp made—12 ch sps)*

Rnd 3: Ch 1, sc in joining ch sp, ch 9, skip next ch sp, (sc in next ch sp, ch 9, skip next ch sp) around, join with sl st in first sc. *(6 ch sps)*

Rnd 4: Ch 1, sc in first st, (5 sc, ch 4, 4 sc) in next ch sp, *(sc, ch 4, sc) in next st, (5 sc, ch 4, 4 sc) in next ch sp; repeat from * around, sc in same st as first sc, ch 2, join with hdc in first sc. *(12 ch sps)*

Rnd 5: Ch 1, sc in joining ch sp, (ch 6, sc in next ch sp) around, ch 6, join with sl st in first sc.

Rnd 6: Sl st in next 2 chs of first ch-6, ch 1, sc in same ch sp, (ch 6, sc in next ch sp) around, ch 3, join with dc in first sc.

Rnd 7: Ch 1, sc in joining ch sp, (ch 9, sc in next ch sp) around, ch 4, join with tr in first sc.

Rnd 8: Ch 1, sc in joining ch sp, (ch 10, sc in next ch sp) around, ch 10, join with sl st in first sc.

Rnd 9: Ch 1, sc in first st, ch 12, (sc in next st, ch 12) around, join.

Rnd 10: (7 sc, ch 3, 7 sc) in each ch-12 sp around, join.

Rnd 11: Sl st in first 7 sts, ch 1, sl st in first ch sp; holding Frame above last rnd, work 25 sc around Frame *(see Stitch Guide—referred to as ring)*, *sl st in next ch-3 sp on last rnd, work 25 sc around Frame; repeat from * around, join with sl st in first ch-3 sp; for **hanging loop,** ch 50, sl st in first ch of ch-50. Fasten off.

Position tops of sc sts on rnd 11 along back of outer edge on Frame, stretching last rnd of crochet piece slightly.

Finishing
1: With white thread, sew heart-shaped bead or button close to center of Catcher in desired position.

2: For **long bead tassel,** thread beading needle with a 12" length of double-strand white and blue thread. String six assorted beads onto thread in desired order, add large glass bead and one seed bead; pull beads to center of thread, skip seed bead and run thread back through glass bead and assorted beads.

3: Using remaining ends of thread, ch 10; sl st in first of the three sl sts at center bottom of Frame. Fasten off. Repeat, making second long bead tassel and join it in third sl st at center bottom of Frame.

4: Working in same manner, make a short bead tassel using five assorted beads and one seed bead and join tassel in second sl st at center bottom of Frame.

5: Glue last two beads to end of large feather and tack or glue feather to one side of Catcher *(see photo)*.

6: Glue three small feathers to bottom of Catcher in front of each bead tassel *(see photo)*. 🏠

Sun & Sea

Finished Size: 6¼" long excluding hanging loop and decoration.

Materials:
- ❏ 150 yds. yellow size 10 crochet cotton thread
- ❏ 1 package narrow medium-size *(2" to 5" long)* bird feathers
- ❏ Beads:
  - 2 clear seed beads
  - 3 gold 4-mm round beads
  - 3 yellow 6 × 22mm spaghetti beads
  - 19 small *(3 to 5mm)* beads in assorted colors and shapes
- ❏ One ¾" shell bead
- ❏ 6" plastic lid *(from whipped topping or large margarine container)*
- ❏ Yellow sewing thread

continued on page 80

Q-Hook Rug

Designed by Carolyn Christmas

Finished Size: 27" × 39".

Materials:
- ❑ Worsted yarn:
  - 14 oz. lt. purple
  - 10½ oz. dk. purple
  - 7 oz. med. purple
- ❑ Tapestry needle
- ❑ Q hook or hook needed to obtain gauge

Gauge: Rnd 1 of Block is 4½" across.

Basic Stitches: Ch, sl st, sc, dc.

Note: Entire Rug is worked with four strands of yarn held together as one.

Block (make 6)

Rnd 1: With med. purple, ch 4, sl st in first ch to form ring, ch 3, 2 dc in ring, ch 2, (3 dc, ch 2) 3 times in ring, join with sl st in top of ch-3. Fasten off.

Rnd 2: Join dk. purple with sl st in any ch sp, (ch 3, 2 dc, ch 2, 3 dc, ch 1) in same sp as joining sl st, (3 dc, ch 2, 3 dc, ch 1) in each ch sp around, join. Fasten off.

Rnd 3: Join lt. purple with sl st in any ch-2 sp, (ch 3, 2 dc, ch`2, 3 dc, ch 1) in same sp as joining sl st, 3 dc in next ch-1 sp, ch 1, *(3 dc, ch 2, 3 dc) in next ch-2 sp, ch 1, 3 dc in next ch-1 sp, ch 1; repeat from * around, join. Fasten off.

Assembly

Holding Blocks wrong sides together, working in **back lps** *(see Stitch Guide)*, with tapestry needle and one strand med. purple, sew Blocks together in two rows of three Blocks each.

Border

Rnd 1: Join dk. purple with sl st in corner ch sp before one long edge, (ch 3, 4 dc) in same sp as joining sl st, *evenly space 30 dc across to next corner ch sp, 5 dc in corner ch space; working across short end, evenly space 18 sc across to next corner ch sp*, 5 dc in next corner ch sp; repeat between first and second *, join with sl st in top of ch-3. Fasten off. *(Third dc of each 5-dc group is corner st.)*

Rnd 2: Join lt. purple with sl st in any corner st, (ch 3, 4 dc) in same st as joining sl st, [*skip next st, sc in next st, (3 dc in next st, skip next st, sc in next st, skip next st) across to next corner st], 5 dc in next corner st, repeat from * 2 more times; repeat between [ ], join. Fasten off.

Rnd 3: Join med. purple with sc in sp between first 2 sts of any 5-dc corner group before one long edge, ch 3, sl st in third ch from hook *(picot made),* ◆(sc between next 2 sts, picot)

continued on page 80

Cupie Doll

Finished Size: 6¼" tall.

Materials:
- ❑ Size 10 crochet cotton thread:
  - 125 yds. lilac
  - 25 yds. each med. purple and cream
- ❑ 1 oz. white worsted yarn
- ❑ Polyester fiberfill
- ❑ 6 beaded dk. purple ribbon bows
- ❑ Small ribbon roses:
  - 2 each off-white or cream and lilac
  - 1 purple
- ❑ 7" square piece of cardboard
- ❑ Hot glue gun and glue
- ❑ 5½" cupie doll
- ❑ Lock of curly doll hair
- ❑ Embroidery needle
- ❑ E hook and No. 7 steel hook or hooks needed to obtain gauges

Gauges: **E hook and yarn,** 5 sc = 1"; 5 sc rows = 1". **No. 7 hook and cotton thread,** 9 sts = 1"; 4 dc rows = 1".

Basic Stitches: Ch, sl st, sc, hdc, dc, tr, dtr.

Stand Form
Bottom (make 2)
Rnd 1: With E hook and white, ch 2, 4 sc in second ch from hook, join with sl st in first sc. *(4 sc made)*

Rnd 2: Ch 3, 3 dc in same st as ch-3, 4 dc in each st around, join with sl st in top of ch-3. *(16 dc)*

Rnd 3: (Ch 3, 2 dc) in first st, dc in next st, (3 dc in next st, dc in next st) around, join. Fasten off. *(32)*

Using crochet piece as pattern, cut one circle from cardboard.

Tube
Rnd 1: Hold wrong side of Bottom pieces together with cardboard piece between, working through both thicknesses, with E hook, join white with sl st in any st on rnd 3, sl st in each st around, join with sl st in first sl st, **turn.** *(32 sl sts made)*

Rnd 2: Ch 1, sc in each st around, join with sl st in first sc, **do not turn.** *(Wrong side of sts are inside of Tube.)*

Rnds 3–4: Ch 1, sc in each st around, join.

Rnds 5–7: Ch 2, hdc in each st around, join with sl st in top of ch-2.

Rnd 8: Ch 3, dc in each st around, join with sl st in top of ch-3. Fasten off.

Dress
Rnd 1: Working this rnd in **back lps** *(see Stitch*

continued on page 78

Lilac Decor

Designed by Claudine Wendt & Maria Nagy

continued from page 76

Guide), with No. 7 hook, join lilac with sl st in first st on rnd 8 of Tube, (ch 3, dc) in same st as joining sl st, 2 dc in each st around, join with sl st in top of ch-3, turn. *(64 dc made)*

Rnd 2: For **Bodice,** working this rnd in **front lps,** ch 3, dc in next st, dc next 2 sts tog, (dc in each of next 2 sts, dc next 2 sts tog) around, join, **turn.** *(48)*

Rows 3–5: Working in rows, ch 3, dc in each st across, turn.

Row 6: Working this row in **front lps,** ch 3, dc in next 6 sts, 2 dc in next st; for **Armhole,** ch 10, skip next 5 sts; dc in next 22 sts; for **Armhole,** ch 10, skip next 5 sts; 2 dc in next st, dc in last 7 sts, turn. *(60 sts and chs)*

Row 7: Working this row in **back lps,** ch 3, dc in next 8 sts, dc next 2 chs tog, dc in next 6 chs, dc next 2 chs tog, (dc in each of next 2 sts, dc next 2 sts tog) 5 times, dc in each of next 2 sts, dc next 2 chs tog, dc in next 6 chs, dc next 2 chs tog, dc in last 9 sts. Fasten off. *(51 dc)*

Rnd 8: For **Skirt,** with top edge of Bodice facing you, working in remaining **back lps** on rnd 1 of Dress, with No. 7 hook, join lilac with sl st in first ch, ch 3, dc in each st around, join with sl st in top of ch-3, **turn.** *(64)*

Rnd 9: Ch 3, 2 dc in next st, (dc in next st, 2 dc in next st) around, join, **turn.** *(96)*

Rnd 10: Ch 3, dc in each st around, join, **turn.**

Rnd 11: Working this rnd in **front lps,** ch 3, dc in each st around, join, **turn.**

Rnd 12: Working this rnd in **back lps,** ch 3, dc in each st around, join, **do not turn.**

Rnd 13: Working this rnd in **back lps,** ch 3, dc in each st around, join, **turn.**

Rnd 14: Working this rnd in **front lps,** ch 3, dc in each st around, join, **turn.**

Rnd 15: Working this rnd in **back lps,** ch 3, dc in each st around, join, **turn.**

Rnd 16: Working this rnd in **front lps,** ch 3, dc next 2 sts tog, (dc in next st, dc next 2 sts tog) around, join, **turn.** Fasten off.

Bottom Ruffle

Rnd 1: With Bodice facing you, working in remaining **front lps** on rnd 14 of Skirt, with No. 7 hook, join med. purple with sc in first st, ch 4, skip next 2 sts, (sc in next st, ch 4, skip next 2 sts) around, join with sl st in first sc. *(32 ch sps made)*

Rnd 2: (Sl st, ch 4, dc, ch 1, dc, ch 1, dc) in first ch sp, (sc; for **picot, ch 3, sl st in third ch from hook;** sc) in next ch sp, *(dc, ch 1, dc, ch 1, dc, ch 1, dc) in next ch sp, (sc, picot, sc) in next ch sp; repeat from * around, join with sl st in third ch of ch-4. Fasten off.

Top Ruffle

Row 1: With bottom of Skirt facing you, working in remaining **front lps** of row 6 on

Bodice, with No. 7 hook, join med. purple with sc in first st, (ch 4, skip next 2 sts, sc in next st) 19 times leaving last 2 sts unworked, turn. *(19 ch sps made)*

Row 2: (Sl st, ch 4, dc, ch 1, dc, ch 1, dc) in first ch sp, *(sc, picot, sc) in next ch sp, (dc, ch 1, dc, ch 1, dc, ch 1, dc) in next ch sp; repeat from * across. Fasten off.

Top Shell

With bottom of Skirt facing you, working in **back lps** of row 7 on Bodice, skip first 21 sts, with No. 7 hook, join cream with sl st in next st, skip next 3 sts, 12 **dtr** *(see Stitch Guide)* in next st, skip next 3 sts, sl st in next st. Fasten off.

Bottom Shell

With top of Bodice facing you, working in remaining **back lps** of row 5 on Bodice, skip first 17 sts, with No. 7 hook, join cream with sc in next st, skip next 4 sts, 12 dtr in next st, skip next 4 sts, sl st in next st. Fasten off.

Sash

Rnd 1: With bottom of Skirt facing you, working in remaining **back lps** of rnd 11 on Skirt, with No. 7 hook, join cream with sc in first st, (ch 34, skip next 31 sts, sc in next st) 2 times, ch 34, join with sl st in first sc, **turn.** *(102 chs made)*

Rnd 2: Working in only one lp of chs and skipping sc sts, (sl st, ch 2) in first ch, hdc in next 5 chs, dc in next 6 chs, tr in next 10 chs, dc in next 6 chs, hdc in next 6 chs, (hdc in next 6 chs, dc in next 6 chs, tr in next 10 chs, dc in next 6 chs, hdc in next 6 sts) 2 times, join with sl st in top of ch-2. Fasten off.

Stuff inside of Skirt firmly around Tube.

Cut 3½"-diameter circle from cardboard. Place circle in bottom of Dress, covering fiberfill.

Glue three ribbon bows over sc sts on Sash. Glue one ribbon bow to center bottom of Top Shell *(see photo).*

Glue one off-white or cream ribbon rose to center of each shoulder.

With embroidery needle and lilac, sew ends of rows on Bodice together. Place doll inside Tube and Bodice.

Hat

Rnd 1: With No. 7 hook and lilac, ch 5, sl st in first ch to form ring, ch 4 *(counts as tr),* 19 tr in ring, join with sl st in top of ch-4, **turn.** *(20 tr made)*

Rnd 2: (Ch 4, tr) in first st, 2 tr in each st around, join, **turn.** *(40)*

Rnd 3: (Ch 4, tr) in first st, 2 tr in each of next 3 sts, tr in next st, (2 tr in each of next 4 sts, tr in next st) around, join, **turn.** *(72)*

Rnd 4: Working this rnd in **front lps,** ch 4, tr in each st around, join, **turn.**

Rnd 5: Working this rnd in **back lps**, ch 4, tr in each st around, join, **turn.**

Rnd 6: Working this rnd in **front lps**, ch 4, tr in each st around, join, **turn.**

Rnd 7: Ch 2 *(counts as hdc)*, hdc in each st around, join with sl st in top of ch-2, **turn.**

Rnd 8: Working this rnd in **back lps**, (ch 4, 2 tr) in first st, 4 tr in each st around, join with sl st in top of ch-4, **turn.** Fasten off.

Cut a strand from lilac to fit around doll's head; weave through sts on rnd 7 of Hat, pull ends to fit around head on doll, secure ends.

Glue two ribbon bows and remaining ribbon roses to side of Hat *(see photo)*. Glue curly hair to inside of Hat centered directly below ribbon roses. Place Hat on doll's head. 🏠

Lamp Shade

Finished Size: 5" across top opening × 8½" long.

Materials:
- ❏ Cotton worsted yarn:
    - 4½ oz. off-white
    - 2 oz. variegated lilac
- ❏ 1 yd. lilac ⅝"-wide satin ribbon
- ❏ 5" diameter × 7" long lamp shade
- ❏ H hook or hook needed to obtain gauge

Gauge: Shell is 1½" wide; 1 tr is 1" tall.

Basic Stitches: Ch, sl st, sc, dc, tr.

Cover

Rnd 1: Starting at top, with off-white, ch 85, sl st in first ch to form ring *(check to make sure ring fits top of shade)*, ch 3, dc in next ch, ch 3, skip next 3 chs, (dc in each of next 2 chs, ch 3, skip next 3 chs) around, join with sl st in top of ch-3. *(17 ch sps made)*

Rnd 2: Sl st in next st, (sl st, ch 1, 2 sc) in first ch sp, ch 4, (2 sc in next ch sp, ch 4) around, join with sl st in first sc.

Rnd 3: For **beginning shell, (beg shell), sl st in next st, (sl st, ch 4, tr, ch 3, 2 tr) in first ch sp;** ch 1; *for **shell, (2 tr, ch 3, 2 tr)** in next ch sp, ch 1; repeat from * around, join with sl st in top of ch-4.

Rnd 4: Beg shell, ch 2, (shell in ch sp of next shell, ch 2) around, join. Fasten off. *(17 shells, 17 ch sps)*

Rnd 5: Join variegated with sl st in any shell, (ch 4, tr, ch 3, 2 tr) in same ch sp, ch 1, 2 tr in next ch-2 sp, ch 1, (shell in next shell, ch 1, 2 tr in next ch-2 sp, ch 1) around, join. *(17 shells, 34 tr)*

Rnd 6: Beg shell, skip next 2 sts of same shell, 2 tr in next tr, ch 3, 2 tr in next tr, (shell in next shell, skip next 2 sts of same shell, 2 tr

in next tr, ch 3, 2 tr in next tr) around, join. Fasten off. *(34 ch-3 sps including shells)*

Rnd 7: Join off-white with sl st in any ch sp, (ch 4, tr, ch 3, 2 tr) in same ch sp as joining sl st, ch 1, (shell in next ch-3 sp, ch 1) around, join. *(34 shells, 34 ch-1 sps)*

Rnd 8: Beg shell, ch 1, 2 tr in next ch-1 sp, ch 1, (shell in next shell, ch 1, 2 tr in next ch-1 sp, ch 1) around, join. *(34 shells, 68 tr)*

Rnd 9: Sl st in next st, sl st in ch sp of first shell, ch 7 *(counts as dtr and ch-2 sp)*, (dtr— *see Stitch Guide,* ch 2) 6 times in same ch sp as last sl st, skip next 2 sts of same shell, sc in each of next 2 tr, ch 2, *(dtr, ch 2) 7 times in ch sp of next shell, skip next 2 sts of same shell, sc in each of next 2 tr, ch 2; repeat from * around, join with sl st in fifth ch of ch-7. Fasten off.

Rnd 10: Join variegated with sc in first dtr; skipping all ch-2 sps and sc, (ch 2, sc in next dtr) 6 times, *sc in next dtr, (ch 2, sc in next dtr) 6 times; repeat from * around, join with sl st in first sc. Fasten off.

Rnd 11: Working in remaining lps on opposite side of starting ch on rnd 1, join variegated with sc in first ch; for **picot**, ch 3, sl st in third ch from hook; sc in next ch, ch 5, skip next 3 chs, (sc in next ch, picot, sc in next ch, ch 5, skip next 3 chs) around, join. Fasten off.

With right side of work facing you, going over two sts and under two sts, weave ribbon through sts on rnd 2; tie ends in bow. 🏠

Q&E Doily

Finished Size: 18" diameter.

Materials:
- ❏ Cotton worsted yarn:
    - 4 oz. variegated lilac
    - 1½ oz. off-white
- ❏ H hook or hook needed to obtain gauge

Gauge: Shell is 1½" wide; 1 tr is 1" tall.

Basic Stitches: Ch, sl st, sc, dc.

Doily

Rnd 1: With variegated, ch 6, sl st in first ch to form ring, ch 3, 15 dc in ring, join with sl st in top of ch-3. *(16 dc made)*

Rnd 2: (Ch 3, dc) in first st, ch 3, skip next st, (2 dc in next st, ch 3, skip next st) around, join. *(16 dc, 8 ch sps)*

Rnd 3: Ch 4, tr in next st; for **shell, (2 tr, ch 3, 2 tr)** in next ch sp; (tr in each of next 2 sts, shell in next ch sp) around, join with sl st in top of ch-4. *(8 shells, 16 tr)*

continued on page 80

Lilac Decor

continued from page 79

Rnd 4: (Ch 4, tr) in first st, ch 3, 2 tr in next tr, ch 1, shell in ch sp of next shell, ch 1, (skip next 2 sts of same shell, 2 tr in next tr, ch 3, 2 tr in next tr, ch 1, shell in ch sp of next shell, ch 1) around, join. *(32 ch sps including shells)*

Rnd 5: For **beginning shell (beg shell), sl st in next st, (sl st, ch 4, tr, ch 3, 2 tr) in first ch-3 sp;** ch 1, 2 tr in next ch-1 sp, ch 1, (shell in next ch-3 sp, ch 1, 2 tr in next ch-1 sp, ch 1) around, join. *(16 shells, 32 tr)*

Rnd 6: Beg shell, ch 2, skip next 2 sts of same shell, tr in each of next 2 tr, ch 2, (shell in next shell, ch 2, skip next 2 sts of same shell, tr in each of next 2 tr, ch 2) around, join.

Rnd 7: Beg shell, ch 1, skip next 2 sts of same shell, 2 tr in next tr, ch 3, 2 tr in next tr, ch 1, (shell in next shell, ch 1, skip next 2 sts of same shell, 2 tr in next tr, ch 3, 2 tr in next tr, ch 1) around, join. *(32 ch-3 sps including shells)*

Rnd 8: Sl st in next st, (sl st, ch 4, tr, ch 5, 2 tr) in first ch-3 sp, ch 1, *(2 tr, ch 5, 2 tr) in next ch-3 sp, ch 1; repeat from *around, join. Fasten off.

Rnd 9: Join off-white with sl st in any ch-5 sp, ch 7 *(counts as dtr and ch-2 sp)*, **(dtr**—*see Stitch Guide*, ch 2) 6 times in same ch sp as joining sl st, sc in next ch-1 sp, ch 2, *(dtr, ch 2) 7 times in next ch-5 sp, sc in next ch-1 sp, ch 2; repeat from * around, join with sl st in fifth ch of ch-7. Fasten off.

Rnd 10: Join variegated with sc in first dtr; skipping all ch-2 sps and sc, (ch 2, sc in next dtr) 6 times, *sc in next dtr, (ch 2, sc in next dtr) 6 times; repeat from * around, join with sl st in first sc. Fasten off. 🏠

Q-Hook Rug

continued from page 75

2 times, *(sc between next 2 sts) 4 times, picot; repeat from * 8 more times, (sc between next 2 sts, picot) 2 times◆, ◊[sc between next 2 sts] 4 times, picot◊; repeat between first and second ◊ 5 more times; repeat between first and second ◆; repeat between first and second ◊ 5 times, (sc between next 2 sts) 3 times, join with sl st in first sc. Fasten off. 🏠

Dream Catchers

continued from page 73

❑ Craft glue
❑ Beading needle
❑ No. 7 steel hook or hook needed to obtain gauge

Gauge: 10 sts or chs = 1"; rnds 1–2 are 1½" across.

Basic Stitches: Ch, sl st, sc, hdc, dc, tr.

Catcher
Note: Being careful not to cut into outer rim, remove the entire center from plastic lid leaving outer rim for Frame.

Rnd 1: Ch 5, sl st in first ch to form ring, ch 1, 7 sc in ring, join with sl st in first sc. *(7 sc made)*

Rnd 2: Ch 1, sc in first st, (ch 10, sc in next st) around, ch 4, join with **ttr** *(see Stitch Guide)* in first sc. *(joining ch sp made—7 ch sps)*

Rnd 3: Ch 1, (sc, ch 4, sc) in joining ch sp, *ch 6, (sc, ch 4, sc) in next ch sp; repeat from * around, ch 2, join with tr in first sc. *(14 ch sps)*

Rnd 4: Ch 1, sc in joining ch sp, ch 8, skip next ch-4 sp, *(sc, ch 5, sc) in next ch-6 sp, ch 8, skip next ch-4 sp; repeat from * around, sc in joining ch sp, ch 1, join with dc in first sc.

Rnd 5: Ch 1, sc in joining ch sp, (ch 8, sc in next ch sp) around to last ch-8 sp, skip ch-8 sp, ch 4, join with tr in first sc. *(13 ch sps)*

Rnd 6: Ch 1, sc in joining ch sp, (ch 8, sc in next ch sp) around, join with sl st in first sc.

Rnd 7: Sl st in first 3 chs of first ch-8, (sl st, ch 3, dc, ch 3, 2 dc) in same ch-8 sp, *ch 6, (2 dc, ch 3, 2 dc) in next ch-8 sp; repeat from * around, ch 6, join with sl st in top of ch-3.

Rnd 8: Sl st in next st, sl st in next ch-3 sp, ch 3; holding Frame above last rnd, work 20 sc around Frame *(see Stitch Guide—referred to as ring),* *dc in next ch-3 sp on last rnd, work 20 sc around Frame; repeat from * around, join with sl st in top of ch-3; for **hanging loop,** ch 20, sl st in first ch of ch-20. Fasten off.

Position tops of sc sts on rnd 8 along outer edge of Frame in a scalloped design, stretching last rnd of crochet piece slightly.

Finishing

1: Thread beading needle with yellow sewing thread. String two seed beads and shell bead onto thread, skip shell bead and run thread back through seed beads. Tack close to center of Catcher in desired position.

2: Arrange feathers in shape of a small wing and tie ends together with a long strand of yellow sewing thread, **do not** cut thread.

3: Thread remaining ends of sewing thread onto beading needle and string on one spaghetti bead; pull ends of feathers into end of bead and string one gold bead onto thread. Position assembled wing on one side of Catcher and using remaining end of thread, tack in place. Glue underside of wing to edge of Catcher.

4: For **long bead tassel,** thread beading needle with a 10" length of yellow sewing thread. String 12 assorted beads onto thread in desired order, add one spaghetti bead and one gold bead; pull beads to center of thread and run thread back through spaghetti and assorted beads. Using remaining ends of thread, tack to bottom of Catcher in desired position.

5: Working in same manner, make a short bead tassel using the remaining beads and tack to bottom of Catcher about ½" from long bead tassel. 🏠

Woodland Dreams

Finished Size: 4¼" long excluding hanging loop and decoration.

Materials:

- ❑ 50 yds. brown size 10 crochet cotton thread
- ❑ 1 package small *(1" to 3" long)* bird feathers
- ❑ 1 orange 4mm round bead
- ❑ 1 orange 12mm cartwheel bead
- ❑ 2" piece beading wire
- ❑ 4" plastic lid *(from margarine container)*
- ❑ Craft glue
- ❑ No. 6 steel hook or hook needed to obtain gauge

Gauge: 8 sts or chs = 1"; rnds 1–2 are 1¼" across.

Basic Stitches: Ch, sl st, sc, hdc, dc, tr.

Catcher

Note: Being careful not to cut into outer rim, remove the entire center from plastic lid leaving outer rim for Frame.

Rnd 1: Ch 10, sl st in first ch to form ring, ch 3, 23 dc in ring, join with sl st in top of ch-3. *(24 dc made)*

Rnd 2: Ch 1, sc in first st, (ch 3, skip next st, sc in next st) around, ch 1, join with hdc in first sc. *(joining ch sp made—12 ch sps)*

Rnd 3: Ch 1, sc in joining ch sp, (ch 4, sc in next ch sp) around, ch 2, join with hdc in first sc.

Rnd 4: Ch 1, sc in joining ch sp, (ch 5, sc in next ch sp) around, ch 2, join with dc in first sc.

Rnd 5: Ch 1, sc in joining ch sp, (ch 6, sc in next ch sp) around, ch 3, join with dc in first sc.

Rnd 6: Ch 1, sc in joining ch sp, (ch 7, sc in next ch sp) around, ch 3, join with tr in first sc.

Rnd 7: Ch 1, sc in joining ch sp, (ch 10, sc in next ch sp) around, join with sl st in first sc.

Rnd 8: Ch 1, sc in first st; holding Frame above last rnd, work 10 sc around Frame *(see Stitch Guide—referred to as ring),* *sl st in fifth and sixth chs of next ch-10 on last rnd, work 10 sc around Frame, sc in next sc on last rnd, work 10 sc around Frame; repeat from * around to last ch-10, sl st in fifth and sixth chs of last ch-10, work 10 sc around Frame, join; for **hanging loop,** ch 20, sl st in first ch of ch-20. Fasten off.

Position tops of sc sts on rnd 8 along center of outer edge on Frame, stretching last rnd of crochet piece slightly.

Finishing

1: Thread round bead onto center of beading wire, bend and twist ends of wire together; thread twisted ends through propeller bead.

2: Placing beads close to center of Catcher in desired position, insert ends of wire through crochet piece and secure in place on back.

3: Arrange clusters of feathers as desired around top and side edge of Catcher and glue in place. 🏠

Lace Frame

Designed by Diane Simpson

Finished Size: 7½" × 9½". Holds 5" × 7" photo.

Materials:
- ❏ 1½ oz. rose worsted yarn
- ❏ 1 oz. off-white fingering yarn
- ❏ 12" × 18" sheet 7-mesh stiff plastic canvas
- ❏ 15" off-white ¼" ribbon
- ❏ Tapestry needle
- ❏ F and G hooks or hook needed to obtain gauge

Gauge: **G hook and worsted yarn,** 4 dc = 1"; 2 dc rows = 1".

Basic Stitches: Ch, sl st, sc, dc.

Cover
Rnd 1: With G hook and rose, ch 90, sl st in first ch to form ring, (ch 3, 2 dc) in first ch, (dc in next 18 chs, 5 dc in next ch, dc in next 25 chs), 5 dc in next ch; repeat betwen ( ), 2 dc in same ch as ch-3, join with sl st in top of ch-3. *(106 dc)*

Rnd 2: (Ch 3, 2 dc) in first st, ***dc back post** *(see Stitch Guide)* around next 22 sts, 5 dc in next st, dc bp around next 29 sts*, 5 dc in next st; repeat between first and second * one more time, 2 dc in same st as ch-3, join. *(122)*

Rnd 3: Ch 3, dc bp around each st around, join. Fasten off.

Rnd 4: Working in starting ch on opposite side of rnd 1, join rose with sc in any st, sc in each st around, join with sl st in first sc. Fasten off.

Lace
Rnd 1: With right side facing you, with F hook and off-white, join with sl st in right-hand corner on one short end, (ch 3, 2 dc, ch 1, 3 dc) in same st as sl st, ch 1, *skip next 4 sts, sc in next st, (ch 3, skip next st, sc in next st) 5 times, ch 1, skip next 3 sts; for **shell, (3 dc, ch 1, 3 dc)** in next st; ch 1, skip next 3 sts, sc in next st, (ch 3, skip next st, sc in next st) 9 times*, ch 1, skip next 3 sts, shell in next st; repeat between first and second * one more time, ch 1, skip last 3 sts, join with sl st in top of ch-3. *(4 shells, 28 ch-3 sps made)*

Rnd 2: Sl st in next 2 sts, (sl st, ch 3; for **picot, ch 3, sl st in third ch from hook;** 2 dc, picot, 2 dc, picot, dc) in ch sp of first shell, *ch 1, skip next ch-1 sp, (sc, picot, sc, ch 1) in each ch-3 sp across to ch-1 sp before next shell, (dc, picot, 2 dc, picot, 2 dc, picot, dc) in ch sp of next shell; repeat from * 2 more times, skip next ch-1 sp, (sc, picot, sc, ch 1) in each ch-3 sp across to last ch-1 sp, skip last ch-1 sp, join. Fasten off.

Frame
From plastic canvas, cut piece 43 × 57 holes for Frame. Leaving 6 holes on each side and 7 holes on top and bottom, cut out center.

For **Back,** cut piece 35 × 45 holes. For **Stand,** cut piece 11 × 30 holes.

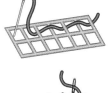

Place Back over cutout on Frame overlapping 2 holes on each side and 1 hole on each end. With off-white, using Running Stitch *(see illustration),* sew together leaving one end open for top.

With bottom of Frame and Stand even, whipstitch *(see illustration)* top of Stand centered to Back with off-white.

Working on center 11 holes on Frame and 4 holes from bottom, insert one ribbon end from front to back into first of 11 holes. Repeat with other ribbon end on last 11 holes. Insert ribbon ends through holes on each side of Stand 4 holes from bottom. Tie ends in bow.

Cut piece rose 18" long. Weave through sts on last rnd of Cover. Place Cover over Frame. Pull yarn tight. Secure ends. 🏠

Spring Hat Wreath

Designed by Sue Childress

Finished Size: Each Flower is about 2¾" across.

Materials:
- ❑ Small amount each of various flower colors, white and green sport yarn
- ❑ Tacky glue
- ❑ Wreath or hat
- ❑ F hook

Basic Stitches: Ch, sl st, sc, hdc, dc.

Flower

Rnd 1: With Flower color, ch 4, sl st in first ch to form ring, ch 3, 14 dc in ring, join with sl st in top of ch-3. *(15 dc made)*

Rnd 2: (Ch 3, 3 dc) in first st, 4 dc in each st around, join. Fasten off.

Rnd 3: Join white with sc in any st, sc in each st around, join with sl st in first sc. Fasten off.

Make as many Flowers as desired to decorate wreath or hat.

Leaf

Row 1: With green, ch 10, dc in third ch from hook, (dc in next ch, 2 dc in next ch) 3 times, dc in last ch, turn.

Row 2: Working in **front lps** *(see Stitch Guide)*, (2 dc in next st, dc in next st) 4 times, hdc in next st, sl st in each of last 2 sts. Fasten off.

Make as many Leaves as desired.

Decorate wreath or hat as desired. 🏠

Fun 'n' Games

Do you think crochet is more than child's play? Not necessarily! If you're young in age or just young at heart, you won't be able to resist the one-of-a-kind kid's creations we've chosen especially with you in mind!

Fun and Games Bag

Designed by Sharon Volkman

Finished Sizes: Bag is 14" wide × 15" high. Checker is 1½" across. Game pieces are 3½".

Materials:
- ❑ Worsted yarn:
  - 9 oz. blue
  - 8½ oz. red
  - 4½ oz. white
- ❑ 2 yarn bobbins
- ❑ Tapestry needle
- ❑ G hook or hook needed to obtain gauge

Gauge: 4 sc = 1"; 4 sc rows = 1".

Basic Stitches: Ch, sl st, sc.

Notes: When **changing colors** *(see Stitch Guide),* drop first color to wrong side of work, pick up again when needed. Always change to next color in last st made. On Checkerboard Side, carefully work each st over dropped color so dropped color does not show on front.

Bag
Checkerboard Side
Row 1: With blue, ch 49, sc in second ch from hook, sc in next 5 chs, (*with red, sc in next 6 chs*; with blue sc in next 6 chs) 3 times; repeat between first and second *, turn. *(24 blue sc, 24 red sc made) Front of row 1 is right side of work.*

Row 2: Ch 1, sc in first 6 sts, (*with blue, sc in next 6 sts*; with red, sc in next 6 sts) 3 times; repeat between first and second *, turn.

Row 3: Ch 1, sc in first 6 sts, (*with red, sc in next 6 sts*; with blue, sc in next 6 sts) 3 times; repeat between first and second*, turn.

Rows 4–6: Repeat rows 2 and 3 alternately, ending with row 2.

Row 7: Join red with sc in first st, sc in next 5 sts, (*with blue, sc in next 6 sts*; with red, sc in next 6 sts) 3 times; repeat between first and second*, turn.

Rows 8–12: Repeat rows 3 and 2 alternately, ending with row 3.

Row 13: Join blue with sc in first st, sc in next 5 sts, (*with red, sc in next 6 sts*; with blue, sc in next 6 sts) 3 times; repeat between first and second *, turn.

Rows 14–18: Repeat rows 2 and 3 alternately, ending with row 2.

Rows 19–48: Repeat rows 7–18 consecutively, ending with row 12. At end of last row, **do not turn.** Fasten off.

Rnd 49: Working around outer edge in sts and ends of rows, join blue with sc in last st made, sc in each st around with 3 sc in each corner, join with sl st in first sc. Fasten off. *(200 sc)*

Note: *Corner st is center st of 3 or 5 sts in corner.*

Rnd 50: Join white with sl st in any corner st, (ch 3, 4 dc) in same st, dc in each st around with 5 dc in each corner st, join with sl st in top of ch-3. Fasten off. *(216 dc)*

Rnd 51: Join red with sc in corner st, 2 sc in same st, sc in each st around with 3 sc in each corner st, join with sl st in first sc. Fasten off.

Tic-Tac-Toe Side
Notes: *Cut 2 strands white each 28 yds. long, wind onto bobbins.*

Work each section of white with separate strand, carry blue across back of work same as for checkerboard side.

Row 1: With blue, ch 49, sc in second ch from hook, sc in next 13 chs; with white, sc in each of next 3 chs; with blue, sc in next 14 chs; with white, sc in each of next 3 chs; with blue, sc in last 14 chs, turn. *(6 white sc, 42 blue sc made)*

Rows 2–14: Ch 1, sc in first 14 sts; with white, sc in each of next 3 sts; with blue, sc in next 14 sts; with white, sc in each of next 3 sts; with blue, sc in last 14 sts, turn. At end of last row, fasten off blue, drop white.

Row 15: Join separate skein white with sc in first st, sc in each st across, turn. *(48 sc)*

Rows 16–17: Ch 1, sc in each st across, turn. At end of last row, fasten off.

Row 18: Join blue with sl st in first st; using white strands dropped from fourth row back, repeat row 2.

Rows 19–48: Repeat rows 2–18 consecutively, ending with row 14.

Rnds 49–51: Repeat rnds 49–51 of Checkerboard Side.

Working through both thicknesses, sew Checkerboard Side and Tic-Tac-Toe Side wrong sides together across sides and bottom.

Top Edging & Drawstring
Rnd 1: Join red with sl st at one side seam, ch 4, skip next st, (dc in next st, ch 1, skip next st) around, join with sl st in third ch of ch-4.

Rnd 2: Ch 1, sc in each st and in each ch around, join with sl st in first sc. Fasten off.

For each **drawstring** *(make 2),* with blue, ch to measure 28". Fasten off.

Starting at one side seam, weave one drawstring through rnd 1 of Top Edging, ending at same seam. Tie ends together. Repeat on opposite side of Bag with other drawstring.

Checker (make 12 red, 12 blue)
Crown Side
Notes: *Do not join rnds unless otherwise stated. Mark first st of each rnd.*

Front side of sts is right side of work.

Rnd 1: With checker color, ch 2, 6 sc in second ch from hook. *(6 sc made)*

Rnd 2: 2 sc in each st around. *(12)*

Rnd 3: (2 sc in next st, sc in next st) around, join with sl st in first sc. Fasten off. *(18)*

continued on page 91

Buckle Up Buddies

Designed by Kathleen Bernier Williford

Buckle-Up Bear

Finished Size: 10" long.

Materials:
- ❑ Worsted yarn:
    - 8 oz. lt. brown
    - Small amount each dk. brown and black
- ❑ 2 brown ⅝" buttons
- ❑ Brown sewing thread
- ❑ Polyester fiberfill
- ❑ Sewing and tapestry needles
- ❑ G hook or hook needed to obtain gauge

Gauge: 4 sc = 1"; 4 sc rows = 1".

Basic Stitches: Ch, sl st, sc.

Body Side (make 2)
Row 1: With lt. brown, ch 15, sc in second ch from hook, sc in each ch across, turn. *(14 sc made)*

Rows 2–5: Ch 1, 2 sc in first st, sc in each st across with 2 sc in last st, turn. At end of last row *(22)*.

Rows 6–26: Ch 1, sc in each st across, turn.

Rows 27–30: Ch 1, sc first 2 sts tog, sc in each st across to last 2 sts, sc last 2 sts tog, turn. At end of last row *(14)*.

Rnd 31: Working around outer edge, ch 1, sc in each st and in end of each row around, join with sl st in first sc. Fasten off.

Hold Body Sides wrong sides together, matching sts; sew together, stuffing before closing.

Head Side (make 2)
Row 1: Starting at top, with lt. brown, ch 13, sc in second ch from hook, sc in each ch across, turn. *(12 sc made)*

Rows 2–5: Ch 1, 2 sc in first st, sc in each st across with 2 sc in last st, turn. At end of last row *(20)*.

Rows 6–16: Ch 1, sc in each st across, turn.

Rows 17–20: Ch 1, sc first 2 sts tog, sc in each st across to last 2 sts, sc last 2 sts tog, turn. At end of last row *(12)*.

Rnd 21: Working around outer edge, ch 1, sc in each st and in end of each row around, join with sl st in first sc. Fasten off.

Muzzle
Row 1: With dk. brown, ch 7, sc in second ch from hook, sc in each ch across, turn. *(6 sc made)*

Rows 2–3: Ch 1, 2 sc in first st, sc in each st across with 2 sc in last st, turn. *(8, 10)*

Rows 4–7: Ch 1, sc in each st across, turn.

Rows 8–9: Ch 1, sc first 2 sts tog, sc in each st

continued on page 90

Buckle Up Buddies

continued from page 89

across to last 2 sts, sc last 2 sts tog, turn. *(8, 6)*

Rnd 10: Working around outer edge, ch 1, sc in each st and in end of each row around, join with sl st in first sc. Fasten off.

Facial Features & Head Assembly

With black, using satin stitch and straight stitch *(see Stitch Guide),* embroider nose and mouth centered over rows 5–8 of Muzzle according to photo.

With matching yarn, sew Muzzle centered over rows 9–17 of Head Side, stuffing before closing.

For **eyes,** sew buttons centered above Muzzle 1" apart.

Hold Head Sides wrong sides together, matching sts; with matching yarn, sew together, stuffing before closing.

Sew rows 6–11 of Head centered over rows 25–30 of Body.

Ear Side (make 4)

Row 1: With lt. brown, ch 5, sc in second ch from hook, sc in each ch across, turn. *(4 sc made)*

Rows 2–3: Ch 1, 2 sc in first st, sc in each st across with 2 sc in last st, turn. *(6, 8)*

Rows 4–6: Ch 1, sc in each st across, turn.

Rnd 7: Working around outer edge, ch 1, sc in each st and in end of each row around, join with sl st in first sc. Fasten off.

For each Ear, hold two Ear Sides wrong sides together, matching sts; sew together.

Sew to seam centered on top of Head ⅝" apart.

Foot Side (make 8)

Row 1: With lt. brown, ch 5, sc in second ch from hook, sc in each ch across, turn. *(4 sc made)*

Rows 2–4: Ch 1, 2 sc in first st, sc in each st across with 2 sc in last st, turn. *(8, 10)*

Rows 5–6: Ch 1, sc in each st across, turn.

Rnd 7: Working around outer edge, ch 1, sc in each st and in end of each row around, join with sl st in first sc. Fasten off.

For each Foot, hold two Foot Sides wrong sides together, matching sts; sew together, stuffing before closing.

Sew two Feet to seam centered on one side of Body 1¼" apart. Repeat on other side of Body.

Seat Belt Loop

Row 1: With lt. brown, ch 11, sc in second ch from hook, sc in each ch across, turn. *(10 sc made)*

Rows 2–25: Ch 1, sc in each st across, turn.

Rnd 26: Working around outer edge, ch 1, sc in each st and in end of each row around, join with sl st in first sc. Fasten off.

Sew long edges of Seat Belt Loop centered lengthwise to bottom of Body leaving short ends unsewn. ❦

Buckle-Up Bunny

Finished Size: 10" long.

Materials:
- ❑ Worsted yarn:
   8 oz. off-white
   Small amount pink
- ❑ 3" pink pom-pom
- ❑ 2 pink ⅝" buttons
- ❑ Pink sewing thread
- ❑ Polyester fiberfill
- ❑ Sewing and tapestry needles
- ❑ G hook or hook needed to obtain gauge

Gauge: 4 sc = 1"; 4 sc rows = 1".

Basic Stitches: Ch, sl st, sc.

Body Side, Head Side & Muzzle

With off-white, work same as Buckle-Up Bear's Body Side, Head Side and Muzzle on page 87.

Facial Features & Head Assembly

With pink yarn and buttons, work same as Buckle-Up Bear's Facial Features and Head Assembly.

Inner Ear (make 2)

Row 1: With pink, ch 17, sc in second ch from hook, sc in next 14 chs, 3 sc in last ch; working in remaining lps on opposite side of starting ch, sc in each ch across, turn. Fasten off. *(33 sc made)*

Row 2: Join off-white with sc in first st, sc in next 14 sts, 2 sc in each of next 3 sts, sc in each st across. Fasten off.

Outer Ear (make 2)

Row 1: With off-white, ch 17, sc in second ch from hook, sc in next 14 chs, 3 sc in last ch; working in remaining lps on opposite side of starting ch, sc in each ch across, turn. *(33 sc made)*

Row 2: Ch 1, sc in first 14 sts, 2 sc in each of next 3 sts, sc in each st across, turn.

Row 3: Hold one Inner Ear and Outer Ear together with Outer Ear facing you, matching sts; working through both thicknesses, ch 1, sc in first 16 sts, (2 sc in next st, sc in next st) 3 times, sc in each st across. Fasten off.

With Inner Ear facing front, sew to seam centered on top of Head ½" apart.

Foot Side & Seat Belt Loop

With off-white, work same as Buckle-Up Bear's Foot Side and Seat Belt Loop.

For tail, sew pom-pom to center back end of Body. ❦

continued from page 87

King Side

Rnd 1: With same checker color, ch 2, 6 sc in second ch from hook, drop yarn, **do not fasten off.** *(6 sc made)*

Rnd 2: Join white with sc in first st, sc in same st, 2 sc in each st around, join with sl st in first sc. Fasten off. *(12)*

Rnd 3: Pick up dropped yarn, sc in first st, 2 sc in next st, (sc in next st, 2 sc in next st) around, join. Fasten off. *(18)*

Sew one King Side and one Crown Side wrong sides together.

X's (make 10)

Rnd 1: With red, ch 8, sc in second ch from hook, sc in next 5 chs, sl st in last ch, (ch 7, sc in second ch from hook, sc in next 5 chs, sl st in same ch of ch-8 as last sl st made) 3 times. *(4 points made)*

Rnd 2: Working around outer edge on opposite side of starting ch and in sts, ch 1, skip next ch, (sc in next 5 chs, 3 sc in side of end st, sc in top of same st, sc in next 4 sts; skipping sl st, sc next st and next ch tog) 4 times, join with sl st in first sc. Fasten off.

For each X, working in **back lps,** sew two X's wrong sides together.

O's (make 10)

Rnd 1: With white, ch 24, sl st in first ch to from ring, 2 sc in first ch, (sc in each of next 3 chs, 2 sc in next ch) 5 times, sc in each of last 3 chs. *(30 sc made)*

Rnd 2: Sc in each of first 3 sts, (2 sc in next st, sc in next 4 sts) 5 times, 2 sc in next st, sc in last st. *(36)*

Rnd 3: (2 sc in next st, sc in next 5 sts) around, join with sl st in first sc. Fasten off. *(42)*

For each O, working in **back lps** *(see Stitch Guide),* sew two O's wrong sides together.

Domino (make 28)

Bottom

Row 1: With blue, ch 7, sc in second ch from hook, sc in each ch across, turn. *(6 sc made)*

Rows 2–12: Ch 1, sc in each st across, turn.

Rnd 13: Working around outer edge in sts and ends of rows, sc in each st around with 2 sc in each corner, join with sl st in first sc. Fasten off.

Top

Work same as Bottom.

With red, using backstitch *(see Stitch Guide),* embroider dividing line between rows 6 and 7.

With white, using straight stitch *(see Stitch Guide),* embroider specified number of X's on each half of each Domino top according to charts below.

Hold one bottom and one top wrong sides together with bottom side facing you; matching sts, working through both thicknesses, join red with sl st in first st on rnd 13, sl st in each st around, join with sl st in first sl st. Fasten off. ✍

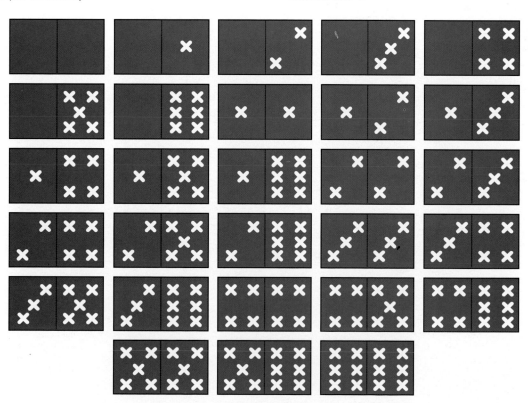

Sampler Rug

Designed by Rosemarie Walter

Finished Size:
21" × 29".

Materials:
❑ Worsted yarn:
7 oz. white
5 oz. red
5 oz. navy
❑ Size 10 crochet cotton thread:
480 yds. white
950 yds. red
❑ Brush-on rug backing
❑ 20¾" × 28¾" piece of felt
❑ Sewing thread to match felt
❑ Sewing needle
❑ H hook or hook needed to obtain gauge

Gauge: 7 sc = 2"; 7 sc rows = 2".

Basic Stitches: Ch, sl st, sc.

continued on page 95

Doll Carrier

Designed by Hope Atwater

Finished Size: 17" long with Straps.

Materials:
- ❑ 3½ oz. worsted yarn
- ❑ Tapestry needles
- ❑ H hook or hook needed to obtain gauge

Gauge: 7 sc = 2"; 9 sc **back lp rows** = 2".

Basic Stitches: Ch, sl st, sc.

Note: Work in **back lps** *(see Stitch Guide)* unless otherwise stated.

Back
Row 1: Ch 13, sc in second ch from hook, sc in each ch across, turn. *(12 sc made)*
Rows 2–16: Ch 1, 2 sc in first st, sc in each st across to last st, 2 sc in last st, turn. At end of last row *(42)*.
Rows 17–32: Ch 1, sc in each st across, turn. At end of last row, fasten off.

Front
Row 1: Ch 13, sc in second ch from hook, sc in each ch across, turn. *(12 sc made)*
Rows 2–12: Ch 1, sc in each st across, turn.
Rows 13–19: Ch 1, 2 sc in first st, sc in each st across to last st, 2 sc in last st, turn. At end of last row *(26)*.
Rows 20–43: Ch 1, sc in each st across, turn. At end of last row, fasten off.

Strap (make 2)
Row 1: Ch 50, sc in second ch from hook, sc in each ch across, turn. *(49 sc made)*
Rows 2–4: Ch 1, sc in each st across, turn. At end of last row, fasten off.

Finishing
Matching sts, sew row 1 at Back and Front together for seam.
Matching ends of rows 18–32 on Back and Front, sew together for side seams.
Sew one end of one Strap across rows 31–34 at side seam.
Sew other end of Strap across four sts at end of row 42 on Front.
Repeat with other Strap.
Front side lays against child's chest. ✎

Sampler Rug

continued from page 93

Notes: Each square on graph = 1 sc.
Wind red yarn into 12 small balls, blue yarn into 11 small balls and white yarn into nine small balls. Wind red crochet cotton into eight small balls and white crochet cotton into seven small balls.
When **changing colors** *(see Stitch Guide),* drop first color to wrong side of work, pick up when needed. Do not carry dropped color along back of work, use separate ball of yarn for each section of color and fasten off each color when no longer needed.
Use one strand of yarn and one strand crochet cotton held together throughout unless otherwise stated.

Rug or Wall Hanging
Row 1: With red yarn and crochet cotton, ch 103, sc in second ch from hook, sc in each ch across, turn. *(102 sc made)*
Rows 2–3: Ch 1, sc in first st changing to white yarn and red crochet cotton, sc in each st across to last st changing to red yarn and red crochet cotton in last st made, sc in last st, turn. *Right side of row 3 is right side of work.*
Rows 4–74: Changing colors according to graph on page 96, ch 1, sc in each st across, turn.
Rnd 75: For **outside trim,** working around outer edge, sl st in each st and in end of each row around, join with sl st in first sl st. Fasten off.
Rnd 76: For **inside trim,** with red yarn and red crochet cotton and right side facing you, holding yarn and crochet cotton at back of work, working over red sts that form inside rectangle, insert hook between any 2 rows or sts, yo, pull through to front, (insert hook between next rows or sts, yo, pull through to front and through lp on hook) around, join with sl st in first sl st. Fasten off.

Finishing
For **wall hanging,** sew felt to back of piece, tack together around inside trim.

continued on page 96

Sampler Rug

continued from page 95

For **rug**, brush back of piece with rug backing. 🪡

☐	= White Yarn/Red Thread
▓	= White Yarn/White Thread
■	= Red Yarn/Red Thread
▒	= Navy Yarn/ White Thread

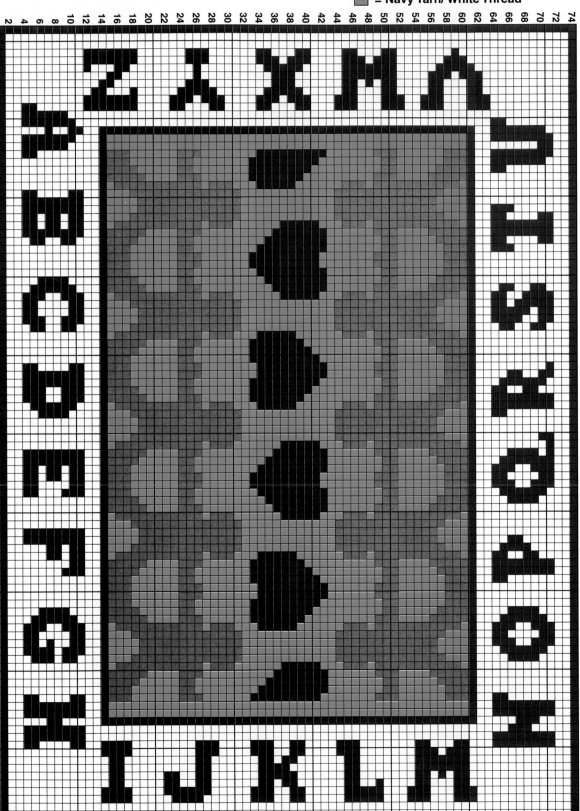

Sampler Rug

Animal Net

Designed by Beth Wood

Finished Size: 33" × 80".

Materials:
- ❑ 500 yds. cotton postal twine
- ❑ H hook or hook needed to obtain gauge

Gauge: 3 mesh = 2"; 3 dc rows = 2".

Basic Stitches: Ch, sl st, sc, dc.

Special Stitches: For **beginning mesh (beg mesh),** ch 5, dc in same st.
For **mesh,** ch 2, skip next 2 chs, dc in next st.
For **end mesh,** ch 2, (dc, ch 2, dc) in third ch of ch-5.

Net
Rnd 1: Ch 2, 6 sc in second ch from hook, join with sl st in first sc. *(6 sc made)*
Row 2: Working in rows, ch 5, dc in next st, ch 2, dc in next st leaving last 3 sts unworked, turn. *(3 dc, 4 chs)*
Row 3: Beg mesh *(see Special Stitches),* **mesh, end mesh,** turn. *(4 mesh)*
Rows 4–40: Beg mesh, mesh across to ch-5, end mesh, turn. At end of last row *(78 mesh).*
Row 41: Ch 5, skip next ch sp, dc in next st, mesh across to ch-5, ch 2, dc in third ch of ch-5, turn.
Rows 42–52: Repeat rows 40 and 41 alternately, ending with row 40. At end of last row, fasten off. *(90 mesh)* ✍

Junior Weight Set

Designed by Cindy Harris

❏ Tapestry needle
❏ J hook or hook needed to obtain gauge

Gauge: Two strands yarn held together, 3 sc = 1"; 2 sc rows = 1".

Basic Stitches: Ch, sl st, sc.

Notes: Work with two strands of yarn held together throughout.
Work in continuous rnds; do not join or turn unless otherwise stated. Mark first st of each rnd.

Preparation

For **Bars,** with handsaw, cut 42" from one broom or mop handle and cut two 16" pieces from other handle.

Bar Cover (make 1 for each Bar)

Rnd 1: With blue, ch 3, sl st in first ch to form ring, ch 1, 2 sc in each ch around. *(6 sc made)*

Rnd 2: (Sc in next st, 2 sc in next st) around. *(9)*

continued on page 101

Finished Sizes: Barbell is 42" long; Dumbbell is 16" long.

Materials:

❏ Worsted yarn:
    24 oz. yellow
    20 oz. blue
    20 oz. red
    16 oz. green
❏ Six 5"-square cardboard pieces
❏ 2 broom or mop handles 1" in diameter or one 42" and two 16" wooden 1" dowels
❏ Polyester fiberfill
❏ Cord elastic
❏ Handsaw

Clowning Around

Designed by Terri Vento

Finished Size: Child's sizes 2–5.

Materials:
- ❑ Worsted yarn:
  - 4½ oz. red
  - Small amount each green and yellow
- ❑ 3" square cardboard
- ❑ G hook or hook needed to obtain gauge

Gauge: 4 sc = 1"; 4 sc rows = 1".

Basic Stitches: Ch, sl st, sc.

Note: Work in continuous rnds; do not join rnds unless otherwise stated. Mark first st of each rnd.

Wig

Rnd 1: With red, ch 2, 8 sc in second ch from hook. *(8 sc made)*

Rnd 2: 2 **lp st** *(see page 66)* in each st around. *(16 lps sts)*

Rnd 3: (2 lp st in next st, lp st in next st) around. *(24)*

Rnd 4: (2 lp st in next st, lp st in each of next 2 sts) around. *(32)*

Rnd 5: Lp st in each st around.

Rnd 6: (2 lp st in next st, lp st in each of next 3 sts) around. *(40)*

Rnd 7: Lp st in each st around.

Rnd 8: (2 lp st in next st, lp st in next 4 sts) around. *(48)*

Rnds 9–10: Lp st in each st around.

Rnd 11: (2 lp st in next st, lp st in next 5 sts) around. *(56)*

Rnds 12–13: Lp st in each st around.

Rnd 14: (2 lp st in next st, lp st in next 6 sts) around. *(64)*

Rnds 15–27: Lp st in each st around. At end of last rnd, join with sl st in first lp st. Fasten off.

Pom Pom Buttons (make 3)

Wrap one strand red around cardboard 30 times; wrap one strand green around same cardboard over red 20 times; wap one strand yellow around same cardboard over green 20 times; slide loops off cardboard; tie separate 8" strand red around center of all loops; cut loops. Trim ends. ✐

Junior Weight Set

continued from page 99

Next Rnds: Work sc evenly around until Cover measures same length as Bar; place Cover over Bar, stretching Cover so the fit is slightly tight *(pull out any extra sts not needed)*.

Last Rnd: (Sc in next st, sc next 2 sts tog) around, join with sl st in first sc. Leaving 8" end for weaving, fasten off.

Weave end through sts on last rnd, pull to close rnd. *(6)*

Large Plate (make 2)
Side A

Rnd 1: With green, ch 14, sl st in first ch to form ring, ch 1, (sc in next ch, 2 sc in next ch) around. *(21 sc made)*

Rnd 2: (Sc in each of next 2 sts, 2 sc in next st) around. *(28)*

Rnd 3: (Sc in each of next 3 sts, 2 sc in next st) around. *(35)*

Rnd 4: (Sc in next 4 sts, 2 sc in next st) around. *(42)*

Rnd 5: (Sc in next 5 sts, 2 sc in next st) around. *(49)*

Rnd 6: (Sc in next 6 sts, 2 sc in next st) around. *(56)*

Rnd 7: (Sc in next 7 sts, 2 sc in next st) around. *(63)*

Rnd 8: (Sc in next 8 sts, 2 sc in next st) around. *(70)*

Rnd 9: (Sc in next 9 sts, 2 sc in next st) around. *(77)*

Rnd 10: (Sc in next 10 sts, 2 sc in next st) around, join with sl st in first sc. Fasten off. *(84)*

Side B

Rnd 1: With wrong side of Side A facing you, working on opposite side of starting ch, join

continued on page 102

Junior Weight Set

continued from page 101

green with sc in first ch on rnd 1, 2 sc in next ch, (sc in next ch, 2 sc in next ch) around. *(21 sc made)*

Rnds 2–10: Repeat rnds 2–10 of Side A.

Matching sts on Side A to Side B, whipstitch last rnds together through both lps, stuffing firmly as you close.

Medium Plate (make 6)

With yellow, repeat rnds 1–8 of Side A. At end of last rnd, join with sl st in first sc. Fasten off. *(70 sc made on last rnd)*

Assemble same as Side A and B of Large Plate.

Small Plate (make 6)

With red, repeat rnds 1–6 of Side A. At end of last rnd, join with sl st in first sc. Fasten off. *(56 sc made on last rnd)*

Assemble same as Side A and B of Large Plate.

Inner Collar (make 6)

Rnd 1: With blue, ch 12, sl st in first ch to form ring, ch 1, (sc in next ch, 2 sc in next ch) around. *(18 sc made)*

Rnd 2: (Sc in each of next 2 sts, 2 sc in next st) around. *(24)*

Rnd 3: (Sc in each of next 3 sts, 2 sc in next st) around, join with sl st in first sc. *(30)*

Rnd 4: Working in **back lps** *(see Stitch Guide),* ch 1, sc in each st around, join.

Rnd 5: Working in **back lps,** ch 1, sc in each of first 3 sts, sc next 2 sts tog, (sc in each of next 3 sts, sc next 2 sts tog) around. *(24)*

Cut circle from cardboard according to Circle pattern piece at right. Place cardboard circle inside crochet piece.

Rnd 6: Working in **both lps,** (sc in each of next 2 sts, sc next 2 sts tog) around. *(18)*

Rnd 7: (Sc in next st, sc next 2 sts tog) around, join with sl st in first sc. Fasten off. *(12)*

Matching sts, whipstitch beginning ch on rnd 1 to last rnd.

Slide one Inner Collar over Bar, 10" from each end of 42" Bar and 4" from each end of each 16" Bar. Tack to secure.

Outer Collar (make 6)

Rnd 1: With blue, ch 14, sl st in first ch to form ring, ch 1, (sc in next ch, 2 sc in next ch) around, join with sl st in first sc. *(21 sc made)*

Rnd 2: Working in **back lps,** ch 1, sc in each st around, join with sl st in first sc.

Rnd 3: Ch 1, sc in first st, sc next 2 sts tog, (sc in next st, sc next 2 sts tog) around. Fasten off. *(14)*

Matching sts, whipstitch beginning ch on rnd 1 to last rnd.

Place Outer Collar over Bar for sizing. Weave cord elastic between sts on rnd 1; pull cord tightly. Secure ends.

Assembly

For **Barbell,** place one each of Large, Medium and Small Plates over each end of 42" Bar, securing Plates with one Outer Collar on each end.

For **Dumbbells,** place one each of Medium and Small Plates over each end of each 16" Bar, securing Plates with one Outer Collar on each end. ✒

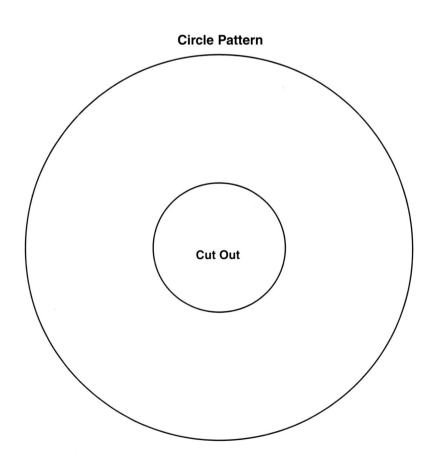

Circle Pattern

Cut Out

Gone to the Dogs!

Chapter Six — Pet Projects to Please Pups!

It's dog's day to play with the picked-for-the-pooch projects in this section! A paradise for pets of all shapes and sizes, this chapter includes pads and pillows, simple sweaters and slippers for man's best friend anywhere!

Paws & Bones

Designed by Ann Parnell

Finished Sizes: Small is 14½" around chest, 14" long; medium is 17" around chest, 16¼" long.

Materials:
- ❏ Worsted yarn:
    - 6 oz. white
    - 1 oz. black
    - Small amount red
- ❏ 4 black 1¼" flat buttons
- ❏ 2 bobby pins for markers
- ❏ Black sewing thread
- ❏ Sewing and tapestry needles
- ❏ F and H hooks or hook needed to obtain gauge

Gauge: H hook, 15 sc = 4"; 9 sc rows = 2"; 5 sc **back lp** rows = 1".

Basic Stitches: Ch, sl st, sc.

Notes: Instructions are for small; changes for medium are in [ ].

When **changing colors** *(see Stitch Guide),* drop first color, pick up when needed. Carry dropped color along back of work.

Top
Row 1: Starting at **tail,** with H hook and white, ch 21, sc in second ch from hook, sc in each ch across, turn. *(20 sc made)*

Rows 2–9 [2–13]: Ch 1, 2 sc in first st, sc in each st across to last st, 2 sc in last st, turn. At end of last row *(36) [44].*

Rows [14–17]: For **medium** only, ch 1, sc in each st across, turn.

Row 10 [18]: For **both sizes,** ch 1, sc in first 7 [11] sts, mark last st made; for row 1 of paw print graph on page 106, sc in each of next 3 sts changing to black in last st made *(see Notes),* sc in each of next 3 sts changing to white in last st made, sc in next 17 sts, mark last st made; sc in last 6 [10] sts, turn. *Front of row 10 [18] is right side of work.*

Rows 11–39 [19–47]: Changing colors according to rows 2–30 of paw print graph between markers, ch 1, sc in each st across, turn. At end of last row, remove markers.

Rows 40–46 [48–54]: Ch 1, sc in each st across, turn.

Row 47 [55]: Ch 1, sc in first 10 sts [14 sts], mark last st made; for row 1 of bone graph on page 106, sc in next st changing to red, (sc in each of next 3 sts changing to white in last st made), sc in next 8 sts changing to red in last st made;

repeat between ( ), sc in each of next 2 sts, mark last st made; sc in last 9 [13] sts, turn.

Rows 48–51 [56–59]: Changing color according to bone graph between markers, ch 1, sc in each st across, turn. At end of last row, remove markers.

Rows 52–53 [60–61]: Ch 1, sc in each st across, turn.

Row 54 [62]: For **first shoulder,** ch 1, sc in first 12 sts leaving last 24 [32] sts unworked, turn. *(12)*

Row 55 [63]: Ch 1, sc first 2 sts tog, sc in each st across, turn. *(11)*

Row 56 [64]: Ch 1, sc in each st across to last 2 sts, sc last 2 sts tog, turn. *(10)*

Row 57 [65]: Ch 1, sc first 2 sts tog, sc in each st across, turn. *(9)*

Row 58 [66]: Ch 1, sc in each st across to last 2 sts, sc last 2 sts tog, turn. *(8)*

Rows 59–67 [67–77]: Ch 1, sc in each st across, turn. At end of last row, fasten off.

Row 54 [62]: For **neck edge,** skip next 12 [20] unworked sts on row 53 [61] for neck opening; for **second shoulder,** join white with sc in next st, sc in each st across, turn. *(12)*

Rows 55–58 [63–66]: Repeat rows 56 and 55 [64 and 63] of first shoulder alternately. At end of last row *(8).*

Rows 59–67 [67–77]: Ch 1, sc in each st across, turn. **Do not fasten off.**

Neck Ribbing
Row 1: Continuing on second shoulder of Top, with H hook and white, ch 9 [11], sc in second ch from hook, sc in each ch across, sl st in next row on Top, turn. *(8 sc made) [10 sc made]*

Row 2: Working in **back lps** *(see Stitch Guide),* ch 1, sc in each st across, turn.

Row 3: Working in **back lps,** ch 1, sc in each st across, skip next row or st, sl st in next row or st, turn.

Rows 4–40 [4–52]: Working in ends of rows and in **both lps** of sts across neck edge to last row on first shoulder, repeat rows 2 and 3 alternately, ending with row 2.

Row 41 [53]: Working in **back lps,** ch 1, sc in each st across, sc in each st across row 67 [77] of first shoulder. **Do not fasten off.** *(16) [18]*

Bottom
Row 1: Continuing with H hook and white, ch 29 [37], sc in second ch from hook, sc in each ch across; working in **back lps,** sc in each st

continued on page 106

Pet Pad

Designed by Peggy Gayron

Finished Size: 21½" across.

Materials:
- ❏ 22 oz. various colors worsted yarn
- ❏ Polyester fiberfill
- ❏ Tapestry needle
- ❏ H hook or hook needed to obtain gauge

Gauge: 7 sc = 2"; 7 sc rows = 2".

Basic Stitches: Ch, sl st, sc.

Notes: Work in continuous rnds; do not join or turn unless otherwise stated. Mark first st of each rnd.

Pad

Rnd 1: With desired color, ch 7, sc in second ch from hook, sc in next 4 chs, 2 sc in last ch; working on opposite side of starting ch, sc in last 5 chs. *(12 sc made)*

Rnds 2–10: Sc in each st around.

Stuff lightly, leaving first 5 rnds unstuffed. Fold tube in half, sew rnds 1–5 to rnds 6–10.

Rnds 11–895: Changing colors *(see Stitch Guide)* as desired, sc in each st around, stuffing and sewing tube together to form circle as you work.

Rnds 896–900: Sc first 2 sts tog, sc in each st around. At end of last rnd, fasten off. *(7)* **Do not stuff** last 2 rnds. Sew opening closed. 🐕

Paws & Bones

continued from page 105

across row 41 [53] of Neck Ribbing, turn. *(44 sc made)* [54 sc made]

Rows 2–28 [2–32]: Working in **back lps,** ch 1, sc in each st across, turn.

Row 29 [33]: For **first flap,** working in **both lps,** ch 1, sc in first 16 [18] sts leaving last 28 [36] sts unworked, turn. *(16)* [18]

Rows 30–33 [34–37]: Ch 1, sc in each st across, turn.

Row 34 [38]: Ch 1, sc in each of first 2 sts; for **buttonhole, ch 3, skip next 3 sts;** sc in next 6 [8] sts, make buttonhole, sc in each of last 2 sts. Fasten off.

Row 29 [33]: For **second flap,** with back side of row 1 facing you, working on opposite side of starting ch on row 1, skip next 12 [18] chs, join white with sc in next ch, sc in last 15 [17] chs, turn. *(16)* [18]

Rows 30–34 [34–38]: Repeat rows 30–34 [34–38] of first flap.

Matching sts, sew last 16 [18] sts of row 28 [32] to Neck Ribbing and second shoulder to form rib.

Edging

With right side facing you, working around outer edge of Top and Bottom, with F hook, join black with sc in any row or st, ch 1, (skip next row or st, sc in next row or st, ch 1) around, join with sl st in first sc. Fasten off.

Sew buttons on Top matching buttonholes. 🐕

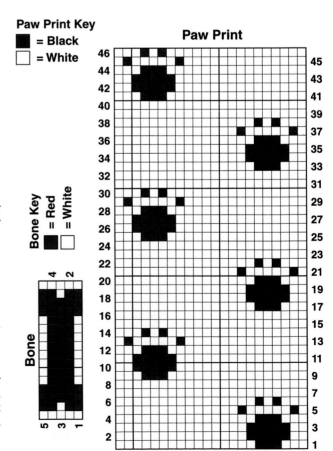

Paw Print Key
- ■ = Black
- □ = White

Bone Key
- ■ = Red
- □ = White

Paw Print

Bone

Dog Coat

Designed by Elizabeth Shute

Finished Sizes: About 15" long; fits most small dogs.

Materials:
- ❑ Small amounts of many colors in worsted yarn
- ❑ Metal ring for button *(Optional—snaps may be used as substitute for button)*
- ❑ G hook or hook needed to obtain gauge

Gauge: Square is 3".

Basic Stitches: Ch, sl st, sc, dc.

Large Square (make 13)
Rnd 1: Ch 5, with sl st in first ch to form ring, ch 3, 2 dc in ring, (ch 3, 3 dc in ring) 3 times, ch 3, join with sl st in top of ch 3. Fasten off. *(4 ch sps made)*

Rnd 2: Join a different color with sl st in any ch sp, ch 3 *(counts as first dc),* (2 dc, ch 3, 3 dc) in same ch sp, (3 dc, ch 3, 3 dc) in each ch sp around, join. Fasten off.

Rnd 3: Join a different color with sl st in any ch sp, ch 3, (2 dc, ch 3, 3 dc) in same ch sp, 3 dc in space between dc groups, *(3 dc, ch 3, 3 dc) in next ch sp, 3 dc in space between dc groups; repeat from * around, join.

Rnd 4: Ch 1, sc in each st and in each ch around, join. Fasten off.

Sew Squares together according to Assembly Diagram #1.

Small Square (make 6)
Rnd 1: Ch 5, sl st in first ch to form ring, ch 3, 2 dc in ring, (ch 3, 3 dc in ring) 3 times, ch 3, join with sl st in top of ch-3. Fasten off. *(4 ch sps made)*

Rnd 2: With joining color, join with sl st in any ch sp, (ch 3, 2 dc, ch 3, 3 dc) in same ch sp, (3 dc, ch 3, 3 dc) in each space around, join.

Sew Squares together according to Assembly Diagram #2.

Finishing
Neck ribbing: join yarn with sl st to neck and working loosely, ch 3, dc in each st around, join with sl st in top of ch-3. Fasten off.

Outer edge: Sc in each st around the outer edge of the coat—excluding neck.

Button: Join yarn with sc in metal ring *(see Stitch Guide),* fill in center with sc, join with sl st in first sc. Fasten off. Sew to end of strap according to diagram.

Loop: Make chain big enough to go over the button. Snaps may be used instead of button and loops. Sew opposite button according to diagram. 🐕

Assembly Diagram #1
Sew top edges together to form neck opening.

Large Squares

Assembly Diagram #2

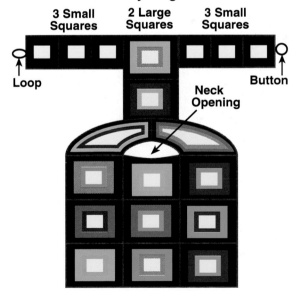

3 Small Squares   2 Large Squares   3 Small Squares

Loop   Button

Neck Opening

Houndstooth

Designed by Michele Maks

Finished Sizes: Small is 18" around chest, 6¼" long including trim; medium is 20" around chest, 8¼" long including trim.

Materials:
- ❑ 3½ oz. each red and black worsted yarn
- ❑ 1¼" Velcro® strip
- ❑ Two 3" decorative safety pins
- ❑ Sewing thread and needle
- ❑ G and H hooks or hook needed to obtain gauge

Gauge: H hook, 7 sc = 2"; 4 sc rows = 1".

Basic Stitches: Ch, sl st, sc, dc.

Notes: Instructions are for small; changes for medium are in [ ].
When **changing colors** *(see Stitch Guide),* drop first color, pick up when needed.

Sweater
Row 1: Starting at **tail,** with H hook and red, ch 50 [56], sc in second ch from hook, sc in each ch across, turn. *(49 sc made) [55 sc made]*

Row 2: Ch 1, 2 sc in first st, sc in each st across to last st, 2 sc in last st changing to black *(see Notes)* in last st made, turn. *(51) [57]*

Row 3: Ch 1, sc in first st, skip first ch of starting ch on row 1, (yo, insert hook in next ch, yo, pull up long lp through ch, complete as dc), sc in next st on row 2, (skip next ch of starting ch on row, yo, insert hook in next ch, yo, pull up long lp through ch, complete as dc, sc in next st on row 2) across, turn.

Row 4: Ch 1, 2 sc in first st, sc in each st across to last st, 2 sc in last st changing to red in last st made, turn. *(53) [59]*

Row 5: Ch 1, sc in first st; working over last 2 rows, yo, insert hook in first st on third row below, yo, pull up long lp through st, complete as dc, sc in next st on last row; *for **long dc (ldc), working over last 2 rows, yo, insert hook in next st in third row below, yo, pull up long lp through st, complete as dc;** sc in next st on last row; repeat from * across, turn.
Note: Work all sc in sts of last row; work all ldc in sc between ldc on third row below.

Row 6: Ch 1, 2 sc in first st, sc in each st across to last st, 2 sc in last st changing to black in last st made, turn. *(55) [61]*

Row 7: Repeat row 5.

Rows 8–15: Repeat rows 4–7 consecutively. At end of last row *(63) [69].*

Row 16: Ch 1, sc in each st across changing to red in last st made, turn.

Row 17: Ch 1, ldc in first st, (sc in next st, ldc in next st) across, turn. For **small** only, fasten off.

Row [18]: For **medium** only, ch 1, sc in each st across changing to black in last st made, turn.

Row [19]: Repeat row 5.

Row [20]: Ch 1, sc in each st across changing to red in last st made, turn.

Row [21]: Repeat row 17.

Rows [22–25]: Repeat rows [18–21]. At end of last row, fasten off.

Row 18 [26]: For **both sizes,** skip first 13 sts, join red with sc in next st, sc in next 32 [42] sts changing to black in last st made leaving last 13 sts unworked, turn. *(37) [43]*

Row 19 [27]: Ch 1, sc first 2 sts tog, ldc in next st, (sc in next st, ldc in next st) 16 [19] times, sc last 2 sts tog, turn. *(35) [41]*

Row 20 [28]: Ch 1, sc first 2 sts tog, sc in each st across to last 2 sts, sc last 2 sts tog changing to red in last st made, turn. *(33) [39]*

Row 21 [29]: Ch 1, sc first 2 sts tog, sc in next st, (ldc in next st, sc in next st) 14 [17] times, sc in next st, sc last 2 sts tog, turn. *(31) [37]*

Row 22 [30]: Ch 1, sc first 2 sts tog, sc in each st across to last 2 sts, sc last 2 sts tog changing to black in last st made, turn. *(29) [35]*

Row 23 [31]: Ch 1, 2 sc in first st, sc in next st, (ldc in next st, sc in next st) 13 [16] times, 2 sc in last st, turn. *(31) [37]*

Row 24 [32]: Ch 1, 2 sc in first st, sc in each st across to last st, 2 sc in last st changing to red in last st made, turn. *(33) [39]*

Row 25 [33]: Ch 1, 2 sc in first st, sc in next st, (sc in next st, ldc in next st) across to last 2 sts, sc in next st, 2 sc in last st, turn. *(35) [41]*

Row 26 [34]: Ch 1, 2 sc in first st, sc in each st across to last st, 2 sc in last st changing to black in last st made, turn. *(37) [43]*

Row 27 [35]: Ch 1, sc in first st, (sc in next st, ldc in next st) 17 [20] times, sc in each of last 2 sts turn.

Row 28 [36]: Ch 1, sc in each st across changing to red in last st made, turn.

Row 29 [37]: Ch 1, sc in first st, (ldc in next st, sc in next st) across, turn.

Row 30 [38]: Ch 1, sc in each st across changing to black in last st made, turn.

Row 31 [39]: For **first side,** ch 1, sc in each of first 2 sts, (ldc in next st, sc in next st) 4 times leaving last 27 [33] sts unworked, turn. *(10)*

Row 32 [40]: Ch 1, sc first 2 sts tog, sc in each st

continued on page 115

Dog Sweater

An Original by Annie

An Original by Annie™

Finished Sizes: Small is 12" long; large is 15" long.

Materials:
- ❑ 4½ oz. fuzzy worsted yarn
- ❑ Tapestry needle
- ❑ H hook or hook needed to obtain gauge

Gauge: 7 sc = 2"; 7 sc rows = 2".

Basic Stitches: Ch, sl st, sc, dc.

Note: Instructions are for small; changes for large are in [ ].

Sweater

Row 1: For **body,** ch 16, [24], sc in second ch form hook, sc in each ch across, turn. *(15 sc made) [23 sc made]*

Row 2: Ch 1, 2 sc in first st, sc in next 5 [9] sts; for **dc cluster (dc cl), yo, insert hook in next st, yo, pull through st, yo, pull through 2 lps on hook, yo, insert hook in same st, yo, pull through st, yo, pull through 2 lps on hook, yo, pull through all 3 lps on hook;** sc in next st, dc cl, sc in last 6 [10] sts, turn. *(16 sts) [24 sts] Front of row 2 is right side of work.*

Row 3: Ch 1, 2 sc in first st, sc in next 6 [10] sts; for **puff st (ps), yo, insert hook in next st, yo, pull long lp through st, (yo, insert hook in same st, yo, pull long lp through st) 2 times, yo, pull through all 7 lps on hook, ch 1, pushing ps to right side of work;** sc in last 8 [12] sts, turn. *(17) [25]*

Row 4: Ch 1, 2 sc in first st, sc in next 5 [9] sts; for **front post cluster (fp cl), yo, insert hook around next dc cl on row before last, yo, pull lp through, yo, pull through 2 lps on hook, yo, insert hook around same dc cl, yo, pull lp through, yo, pull through 2 lps on hook, yo, pull through all 3 lps on hook;** sc in each of next 3 sts, fp cl, sc in last 6 [10] sts, turn. *(18) (26)*

Row 5: Ch 1, 2 sc in first st, sc in next 6 [10] sts, ps, sc in next st, ps, sc in last 8 [12] sts, turn. *(19) [27]*

Row 6: Ch 1, 2 sc in first st, dc in next st, sc in next 4 [8] sts, fp cl, sc in next 5 sts, fp cl, sc in next 4 [8] sts, dc in next st, sc in last st, turn. *(20) [28]*

Row 7: Ch 1, 2 sc in first st, sc in next 6 [10] sts, (ps, sc in next st) 3 times, sc in last 7 [11] sts, turn. *(21) [29]*

Row 8: Ch 1, 2 sc in first st, sc in next st, **front post (fp**—*see Stitch Guide)* around next dc on row before last, sc in each of next 3 [7] sts, fp cl, sc in next 7 sts, fp cl, sc in each of next 3 [7] sts, fp around next dc on row before last, sc in each of last 2 sts, turn. *(22) [30]*

Row 9: Ch 1, 2 sc in first st, sc in next 8 [12]

continued on page 114

Dog Sweater

continued from page 113

sts, ps, sc in next st, ps, sc in last 10 [14] sts, turn. *(23) [31]*

Row 10: Ch 1, 2 sc in first st, sc in each of next 2 sts, fp around next fp on row before last, sc in next 4 [8] sts, fp cl, sc in next 5 sts, fp cl, sc in next 4 [8] sts, fp around next fp on row before last, sc in each of last 3 sts, turn. *(24) [32]*

Row 11: Ch 1, 2 sc in first st, sc in next st; for **berry stitch (bs), insert hook in next st, yo, pull through st *(2 lps on hook, keep first lp on hook);* working in second lp only, ch 3; yo, pull through 2 lps on hook, pushing bs to right side of work;** sc in next 8 [12] sts, ps, sc in next 8 [12] sts, bs, sc in each of last 3 sts, turn. *(25) [33]*

Row 12: Ch 1, 2 sc in first st, sc in each of next 3 sts, fp around next fp on row before last, sc in next 6 [10] sts, fp cl, sc in next st, fp cl, sc in next 6 [10] sts, fp around next fp on row before last, sc in last 4 sts, turn. *(26) [34]*

Row 13: Ch 1, 2 sc in first st, sc in next st, bs, sc in next 9 [13] sts, ps, sc in next 9 [13] sts, bs, sc in each of last 3 sts, turn. *(27) [35]*

Row 14: Ch 1, 2 sc in first st, dc in next st, sc in each of next 3 sts, fp around next fp on row before last, sc in next 5 [9] sts, fp cl, sc in each of next 3 sts, fp cl, sc in next 5 [9] sts, fp around next fp on row before last, sc in each of next 3 sts, dc in next st, sc in last st, turn. *(28) [36]*

Row 15: Ch 1, 2 sc in first st, sc in next st, bs, sc in next st, bs, sc in next 7 [11] sts, ps, sc in next st, ps, sc in next 7 [11] sts, bs, sc in next st, bs, sc in each of last 3 sts, turn. *(29) [37]*

Row 16: Ch 1, sc in each of first 2 sts; for **front post pattern (fp pat), fp around next dc or fp on row before last, sc in each of next 3 sts, fp around next fp or dc on row before last;** sc in next 4 [8] sts, fp cl, sc in next 5 sts, fp cl, sc in next 4 [8] sts, fp pat, sc in each of last 2 sts, turn.

Row 17: Ch 1, sc in first 4 sts, bs, sc in next 7 [11] sts, (ps, sc in next st) 3 times, sc in next 6 [10] sts, bs, sc in last 4 sts, turn.

Row 18: Ch 1, sc in each of first 2 sts, fp pat, sc in each of next 3 [7] sts, fp cl, sc in next 7 sts, fp cl, sc in each of next 3 [7] sts, fp pat, sc in each of last 2 sts, turn.

Row 19: Ch 1, sc in each of first 3 sts, bs, sc in next st, bs, sc in next 7 [11] sts, ps, sc in next st, ps, sc in next 7 [11] sts, bs, sc in next st, bs, sc in each of last 3 sts, turn.

Row 20: Ch 1, sc in each of first 2 sts, fp pat, sc in next 4 [8] sts, fp cl, sc in next 5 sts, fp cl, sc in next 4 [8] sts, fp pat, sc in each of last 2 sts, turn.

Row 21: Ch 1, sc in first 4 sts, bs, sc in next 9 [13] sts, ps, sc in next 9 [13] sts, bs, sc in last 4 sts, turn.

Row 22: Ch 1, sc in each of first 2 sts, fp pat, sc in next 6 [10] sts, fp cl, sc in next st, fp cl, sc in next 6 [10] sts, fp pat, sc in each of last 2 sts, turn.

Row 23: Ch 1, sc in each of first 2 sts, bs, sc in next st, bs, sc in next 8 [12] sts, ps, sc in next 8 [12] sts, bs, sc in next st, bs, sc in each of last 2 sts, turn.

Row 24: Ch 1, sc in each of first 2 sts, fp pat, sc in next 5 [9] sts, fp cl, sc in each of next 3 sts, fp cl, sc in next 5 [9] sts, fp pat, sc in each of last 2 sts, turn.

Row 25: Ch 1, sc in first 4 sts, bs, sc in next 8 [12] sts, ps, sc in next st, ps, sc in next 8 [12] sts, bs, sc in last 4 sts, turn.

Row 26: Repeat row 16.

Row 27: Ch 1, sc in each of first 3 sts, bs, sc in next st, bs, sc in next 6 [10] sts, (ps, sc in next st) 3 times, sc in next 5 [9] sts, bs, sc in next st, bs, sc in each of last 3 sts, turn.

Row 28: Repeat row 18.

Row 29: Repeat row 25.

Row 30: Repeat row 20.

Row 31: Repeat row 23.

Row 32: Repeat row 22.

Row 33: Repeat row 21.

Row 34: Repeat row 24.

Row 35: Repeat row 19.

Rows 36–42 [36–45]: Repeat rows 16–22 [16–25].

Row [46]: For **large** only, repeat row 16.

Row [47]: Repeat row 27.

Row [48]: Repeat row 18.

Row [49]: Repeat row 25.

Row [50]: Repeat row 20.

Row [51]: Repeat row 23.

Row [52]: Repeat row 22.

Row 43 [53]: For **first chest strap,** ch 1, sc in each of first 3 sts, bs, sc in next st, bs, sc in each of next 3 sts leaving remaining sts unworked, turn. *(9)*

Row 44 [54]: Ch 1, sc in each of first 2 sts, fp around next fp on row before last, sc in each of next 3 sts, fp around next fp on row before last, sc in each of last 2 sts, turn.

Row 45 [55]: Ch 1, sc in first 4 sts, ps, sc in last 4 sts, turn.

Row 46 [56]: Ch 1, sc in each of first 2 sts, fp around next fp on row before last, sc in each of next 3 sts, fp around next fp on row before last, sc in each of last 2 sts, turn.

Row 47 [57]: Ch 1, sc in each of first 3 sts, bs, sc in next st, bs, sc in each of last 3 sts, turn.

Rows 48–56 [58–72]: Or to length needed to fit; repeat rows 44–47 [54–57] consecutively, ending with row 44 [56].

Row 57 [73]: Ch 1, sc in each of first 3 sts; for **buttonhole,** ch 5, skip next 3 sts; sc in each of last 3 sts, turn.

Row 58 [74]: Ch 1, sc in each st and in each ch across, turn. Fasten off.

Row 43 [53]: For **second chest strap,** with wrong side facing you, skip next 11 [19] sts on row 42 [52], join with sc in next st, sc in each of next

2 sts, bs, sc in next st, bs, sc in each of last 3 sts, turn. *(9)*

Rows 44–57 [54–73]: Or to length needed to fit, repeat rows 44–47 [54–57] of first strap consecutively, ending with row 45 [57].

Row 58 [74]: Ch 1, sc in each st across. Fasten off.

Bottom Strap

Row 1: Ch 14, sc in second ch from hook, sc in each ch across, turn. *(13 sc made)*

Rows 2–22 [2–29]: Or to length needed to fit; ch 1, sc in each st across, turn.

Row 23 [30]: Ch 1, sc in first 5 sts; for **buttonhole**, ch 5, skip next 3 sts; sc in last 5 sts, turn.

Row 24 [31]: Ch 1, sc in each st and in each ch across, turn. *(15)*

Row 25 [32]: Ch 1, sc in each st across. Fasten off.

Sew row 1 centered to right-hand edge of Sweater body.

Button (make 2)

Rnd 1: With two strands held together, ch 4, 5 dc in fourth ch from hook, join with sl st in top of ch-3. *(6 dc made) First 3 chs count as first dc.*

Rnd 2: Ch 1, sc first 2 sts tog, (sc next 2 sts tog) around, join with sl st in first sc. Fasten off.

Finishing

Sew one Button to left side of Sweater opposite buttonhole on Bottom Strap.

Sew other Button to end of second chest strap opposite buttonhole. 🐕

Houndstooth

continued from page 110

across to last st, 2 sc in last st changing to red in last st made, turn.

Row 33 [41]: Ch 1, sc in each of first 2 sts, (ldc in next st, sc in next st) across, turn.

Row 34 [42]: Ch 1, sc first 2 sts tog, sc in each st across to last st, 2 sc in last st changing to black in last st made, turn.

Rows 35–36 [43–44]: Repeat rows 33 and 32 [41 and 40].

Rows 37–38 [45–46]: Repeat rows 33–34 [41–42].

Row 39 [47]: Repeat row 33 [41].

Row [48]: For **medium** only, ch 1, sc in each st across changing to red in last st made, turn.

Row [49]: Repeat row [41].

Row [50]: Ch 1, sc in each st across changing to black in last st made, turn.

Row [51]: Ch 1, sc in first st, ldc in next st, (sc in next st, ldc in next st) across, turn.

Row 40 [52]: For **both sizes**, ch 1, 2 sc in first st, sc in each st across to last 2 sts, sc last 2 sts tog changing to red in last st made, turn.

Row 41 [53]: Repeat row 33 [41].

Row 42 [54]: Ch 1, 2 sc in first st, sc in each st across to last 2 sts, sc last 2 sts tog changing to black in last st made, turn.

Row 43 [55]: Repeat row 33 [41].

Row 44 [56]: Repeat row 40 [52].

Row 45 [57]: Repeat row 33 [41].

Row 46 [58]: Repeat row 42 [54]. Fasten off red.

Row 47 [59]: Repeat row 33 [41].

Row 48 [60]: Ch 1, 2 sc in first st, sc in each st across to last 2 sts, sc last 2 sts tog, turn.

Row 49 [61]: Ch 1, sc in each st across, turn.

Rows 50–53 [62–65]: Repeat rows 48–49 [60–61]

alternately. At end of last row, fasten off.

Row 31 [39]: For **neck opening**, skip next 17 [23] unworked sts on row 30 [38]; for **second side,** join black with sc in next st, (ldc in next st, sc in next st) 4 times, sc in last st, turn. *(10)*

Row 32 [40]: Ch 1, 2 sc in first st, sc in each st across to last 2 sts, sc last 2 sts tog, turn.

Row 33 [41]: Ch 1, sc first 2 sts tog, sc in each st across to last st, 2 sc in last st. Fasten off.

Edging

Rnd 1: With right side of work facing you, working in ends of rows, in sts and on opposite side of starting ch on row 1, with G hook, join black with sc in first st on row 53 [65] of first side, 2 sc in same st, sc in each st, in end of each row and in each ch around with 3 sc in each corner st, join with sl st in first sc, **turn.**

Rnd 2: Ch 1, sc in each st around with 3 sc in each corner, join. Fasten off.

Finishing

For each **Fringe** *(see Stitch Guide),* cut two strands black each 3½" long; with both strands held together, fold in half, insert hook through st, pull fold through st, pull ends through fold, tighten.

Fringe in each st around leaving neck opening unfringed.

Sew half of Velcro® strip over ends of rows 13–17 [22–26] and second half at opposite ends of same rows to fit around chest.

Place last 8 rows of first side over second side, pin in place with decorative pins. 🐕

Finished Size: 10" wide × 15" long × 9¾" tall.

Materials:
- ❏ 15 oz each blue and red worsted yarn
- ❏ Polyester batting
- ❏ Red quilting thread
- ❏ Tapestry and sewing needles
- ❏ H hook or hook needed to obtain gauge

Gauge: 7 sc = 2"; 7 sc rows = 2".

Basic Stitches: Ch, sl st, sc.

Note: Use two strands yarn held together unless otherwise stated.

Sole (make 1 red, 1 blue)
Row 1: Ch 17, 2 sc in second ch from hook, sc in each ch across to last ch, 2 sc in last ch, turn. *(18 sc made)*

Rows 2–5: Ch 1, 2 sc in first st, sc in each st across to last st, 2 sc in last st, turn. At end of last row *(26).*

Row 6: Ch 1, sc in each st across, turn.

Row 7: Ch 1, 2 sc in first st, sc in each st across to last st, 2 sc in last st, turn. *(28)*

Rows 8–9: Repeat rows 6–7. *(30)*

Rows 10–45: Ch 1, sc in each st across, turn.

Row 46: Ch 1, sc first 2 sts tog, sc in each st across to last 2 sts, sc last 2 sts tog, turn. *(28)*

Row 47: Ch 1, sc in each st across, turn.

Rows 48–52: Ch 1, sc first 2 sts tog, sc in each st across to last 2 sts, sc last 2 sts tog, **do not turn.** At end of last row *(18).*

Rnd 53: Working around outer edge, ch 1, sc in each st and in end of each row around with 2 sc in each corner st, join with sl st in first sc. Fasten off. *Front of rnd 53 is right side of work.*

For **padding,** using one crochet piece as pattern, cut two pieces from batting, trim ¼" smaller on all edges.

With quilting thread, baste padding pieces to wrong side of red Sole.

Hold Soles wrong sides together, with padding between; with single strand blue, matching sts, working through **back lps** *(see Stitch Guide),* sew matching lps together leaving outer front lps unsewn.

Side (make 2 red, 2 blue)
Row 1: Starting at **heel,** ch 22, sc in second ch from hook, sc in each ch across, turn. *(21 sc made)*

Row 2: Ch 1, sc in each st across, turn.

Row 3: Ch 1, sc first 2 sts tog, sc in each st across, turn. *(20)*

Rows 4–5: Repeat rows 2–3. *(19)*

Rows 6–7: Ch 1, sc in each st across, turn.

Rows 8–11: Repeat rows 2 and 3 alternately. At end of last row *(17).*

continued on page 118

An *Original* by *Annie*™

Sleepy Slipper

An Original by Annie

Sleepy Slipper

continued from page 116

Rows 12–40: Ch 1, sc in each st across, turn.
Row 41: Ch 1, 2 sc in first st, sc in each st across, turn. *(18)*
Row 42: Ch 1, sc in each st across to last st, 2 sc in last st, turn. *(19)*
Row 43: Ch 1, sc in each st across, turn.
Row 44: Ch 1, sc in each st across to last 2 sts, sc last 2 sts tog, turn. *(18)*
Row 45: Ch 1, sc in each st across, turn.
Rows 46–49: Repeat rows 44 and 45 alternately. At end of last row *(16)*.
Rows 50–59: Repeat rows 2 and 3 alternately. At end of last row *(11)*.
Rows 60–72: Ch 1, sc in each st across, turn. At end of last row, fasten off.

Vamp (make 1 red, 1 blue)

Row 1: Starting at **toe**, ch 10, sc in second ch from hook, sc in each ch across, turn. *(9 sc made)*
Rows 2–4: Ch 1, 2 sc in first st, sc in each st across to last st, 2 sc in last st, turn. *(15)*
Row 5: Ch 1, sc in each st across, turn.
Row 6: Ch 1, 2 sc in first st, sc in each st across to last st, 2 sc in last st, turn. *(17)*
Rows 7–10: Repeat rows 5 and 6 alternately. At end of last row *(21)*.
Rows 11–13: Ch 1, sc in each st across, turn.
Row 14: Ch 1, 2 sc in first st, sc in each st across to last st, 2 sc in last st, turn. *(23)*
Rows 15–20: Ch 1, sc in each st across, turn.
Row 21: Ch 1, 2 sc in first st, sc in each st across to last st, 2 sc in last st, turn. *(25)*
Rows 22–27: Ch 1, sc in each st across, turn.
Row 28: Ch 1, sc first 2 sts tog, sc in each st across to last 2 sts, sc last 2 sts tog, turn. *(23)*
Row 29: Ch 1, sc in each st across, turn.
Rows 30–34: Ch 1, sc first 2 sts tog, sc in each st across to last 2 sts, sc last 2 sts tog, turn. At end of last row, fasten off. *(13)*
Row 35: Working around **toe**, join with sc in end of row 13, sc in each row and in each ch on opposite side of starting ch on row 1 across to other end of row 13. Fasten off.

Assembly

For **padding**, using red Side and Vamp pieces as patterns, cut one Vamp and two Sides from batting, trim ¼" smaller on all edges. With quilting thread, baste padding pieces to matching red pieces.

Matching sts on red Side pieces, sew heels together and toes together. Working across curved edges on Side, match center of last row on Vamp to toe seam and end of row 23 on Vamp to row 44 on Sides; with red yarn, sew Vamp to Sides. Repeat with blue pieces.

Matching heel seam on Sides to center of row 1 on Sole and toe seam to center of row 72 on Sole, sew straight edge of red Side to unsewn outer front lps on red Sole. Repeat with blue Side and blue Sole.

Trim

Working through both thicknesses in ends of rows and in sts around edge, join red with sc in heel seam, sc in each row and in each st around, join with sl st in first sc. Fasten off.

For **shoelace**, with single strand red, ch to measure 1 yd. Fasten off.

Lacing through sts, starting between rows 14 and 15 on Vamp, leaving 14" end, weave in at 1 and out at 2 *(see illustration)*, in at 3 and out at 4, in at 5 and out at 6, in at 7 and out at 8; tie in bow.

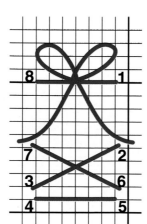

Shoe Lace Key
☐ = Sc Stitch
■ = Shoe Lace

Fabulous Fashions

If the final touch sometimes becomes the final straw, you need the ease and elegance of new and unique accessories! In the next few pages you'll find ways that you can look like a million bucks for only pennies—what a bargain price!

Fabulous Fashions

Circular Shawl

Designed by Teena Parziale

Finished Sizes: Lady's small; changes for large are in [ ].

Materials:
- 24 oz. sport yarn
- K hook or hook needed to obtain gauge

Gauge: 4 tr, 3 ch-1 = 3", 5 rows = 3".

Basic Stitches: Ch, sl st, tr.

Special Stitches: For **beginning increase (beg inc)**, sl st in next st, ch 4, 2 tr in same st, ch 1.
For **increase (inc)**, skip next st, 3 tr in next st, ch 1.
For **mesh**, (tr, ch 1) in ch-1 sp.
For **shell**, (2 tr, ch 2, 2 tr, ch 1) in specified place.
For **beginning shell (beg shell)**, sl st in next st, sl st in next ch sp, (ch 4, tr, ch 2, 2 tr) in same ch sp, ch 1.

Shawl

Rnd 1: Ch 5, 11 tr in fifth ch from hook, join with sl st in top of ch-5. *(12 tr made)*

Rnd 2: (Ch 4, 2 tr) in first st, ch 1, tr in next st, ch 1, (3 tr in next st, ch 1, tr in next st, ch 1) around, join with sl st in top of ch-4. *(24 tr)*

Rnd 3: Beg inc *(see Special Stitches)*, *skip next st, (tr in next ch-1 sp, ch 1) 2 times, **inc** *(see Special Stitches)*; repeat from * around, join. *(30 tr)*

Note: Sts between increases form panels.

Rnds 4–9 [4–11]: Beg inc, **mesh** *(see Special Stitches)* across panel, (inc, mesh across panel) around, join. At end of last rnd, *(66 tr) [78 tr]*.

Rnd 10 [12]: Beg inc, mesh across panel, inc; *for **armhole**, loosely ch 19 [23], skip next panel, skip next st, inc*; (mesh across panel, inc) 2 times; repeat between first and second *, mesh across panel, join. *(54 tr, 38 chs) [62 tr, 46 chs]*

Rnd 11 [13]: Beg inc, mesh across panel, inc, *mesh in next ch, (skip next ch, mesh in next ch) across armhole, inc*, (mesh across panel, inc) 2 times; repeat between first and second *, mesh across panel, join. *(78 tr) [90 tr]*

Rnds 12–23 [14–23]: Beg inc, mesh across panel, (inc, mesh across panel) around, join. At end of last rnd *(150 tr)*.

Rnd 24: Sl st in next st, (ch 4, tr, ch 2, 2 tr) in same st, ch 1, mesh in next 5 ch-1 sps, **shell** *(see Special Stitches)* in next ch-1 sp, (mesh in next 5 ch-1 sps, shell in next ch sp) 2 times, mesh in next 5 ch-1 sps, *shell in center st of next inc, (mesh in next 5 ch-1 sps, shell in next ch sp) 3 times, mesh in next 5 ch-1 sps; repeat from * around, join. *(60 tr, 24 shells)*

Rnds 25–29: Beg shell *(see Special Stitches)*, mesh in each ch sp across to next shell, (shell in next shell, mesh in each ch sp across to next shell) around, join.

Rnd 30: Beg shell, shell in next ch-1 sp, (ch 1, skip next ch sp, shell in next ch sp) across to next shell, *shell in next shell, ch 1, shell in next ch sp, (ch 1, skip next ch sp, shell in next ch sp) across to next shell; repeat from * around, join. *(168 shells)*

Rnds 31–34: Beg shell, (shell in next shell, ch 1) around, join.

Rnd 35: Sl st in next st, (sl st, ch 4, 2 tr) in next shell; for **picot, ch 4, sl st in third ch from hook, ch 1;** 3 tr in same shell as last tr, ch 1, (3 tr, picot, 3 tr, ch 1) in each shell around, join. Fasten off.

Eyelet Lace Vest

Designed by Dorothy Helms

Finished Sizes: Girl's size 2. Changes for 3 and 4 are in [ ].

Materials:
- ❑ 150 yds. of ¾" flat lace
- ❑ ⅔ yd. of ½" satin ribbon
- ❑ Sewing needle and thread to match lace and ribbon
- ❑ P/16 wood hook or hook needed to obtain gauge

Gauge: 6 V sts = 7"; 5 V st rows = 4".

Basic Stitches: Ch, sl st, sc, dc.

Special Stitches: For **V stitch (V st),** 2 dc in next st.

For **beginning V stitch (beg V st),** sl st in first V st, (ch 3, dc) in same st.

Note: When joining new piece of lace, sew ends of last piece and new piece together.

Vest
Row 1: Ch 36 [40, 42], sc in second ch from hook, sc in each ch across, turn. *(35 sc made) [39 sc made, 41 sc made]*

Row 2: Ch 3, skip next st, (**V st**—*see Special Stitches,* skip next st) across to last st, dc in last st, turn. *(16 V sts, 2 dc) [18 V sts, 2 dc; 19 V sts, 2 dc]*

Rows 3–7: Ch 3, V st in each V st across to last st, dc in second ch of ch-3, turn.

Row 8: For **left front,** ch 3, (V st in next V st) 3 times leaving last 13 [15, 16] V sts and last dc unworked, turn. *(3 V sts, 1 dc)*

Row 9: Beg V st *(see Special Stitches),* V st in each of last 2 V sts, dc in top of ch-3, turn.

Row 10: Ch 2, dc in first V st, V st in each V st across, turn. *(2 V sts, 1 dc)*

Row 11: Beg V st, V st in next V st, dc in next dc leaving ch-2 unworked, turn.

Row 12: Ch 3, V st in each V st across, turn.

Row 13: Beg V st, V st in next V st, dc in second ch of ch-3, turn.

Row 14: Ch 3, V st in each V st across. Leaving 8" for sewing, fasten off.

Row 8: For **back,** skip next 2 [3, 3] unworked V sts on row 7, join with sl st in next V st, ch 3, dc in same st, (V st in next V st) 5 [5, 6] times leaving last 5 [6, 6] V sts and last dc unworked, turn. *(6 V sts) [6 V sts, 7 V sts]*

Rows 9–13: Beg V st, V st in each V st across, turn.

Row 14: For **left shoulder,** beg V st, V st in next V st leaving last 4 [4, 5] V sts unworked, turn. *(2 V sts)*

Row 15: Beg V st, V st in last V st. Fasten off.

Row 14: For **right shoulder,** skip each of next 2 [2, 3] V sts, join with sl st in next V st, ch 3, dc in same st, V st in last V st, turn. *(2 V sts)*

Row 15: Beg V st, V st in last V st. Fasten off.

Row 8: For **right front,** skip each of next 2 [3, 3] unworked V sts on row 7, join with sl st in next V st, ch 3, dc in same st, V st in next V st, dc in next V st, dc same sp and second ch of ch-3 tog, turn. *(2 V sts, 2 dc)*

Row 9: Ch 2, V st in first sp, V st in each V st across, turn. *(3 V sts)*

Row 10: Beg V st, V st in next V st, dc next V st and top of ch-2 tog, turn. *(4 V sts, 1 dc)*

Row 11: Ch 3, V st in each V st across, turn.

Row 12: Beg V st, V st in next V st, dc in second ch of ch-3, turn.

Rows 13–14: Repeat rows 11 and 12 of right front. Leaving 8" for sewing, fasten off.

Matching sts, sew front to back at shoulders.

Trim
Starting at back of neck, sew bound edge of lace along entire outside edge of Vest, gathering slightly to ruffle.

Starting at bottom of each armhole, repeat outside trim.

Cut ribbon in half. Sew one end of one piece to inside right front edge at end of row 9. Repeat on left front edge. Tie in bow. ❦

Crochet Hat Trim

Designed by Marie Jones

Finished Size: Fits 22"-23" hat crown.

Materials:
- ❑ 175 yds. white size 10 crochet cotton thread
- ❑ Crownless wide-brimmed hat 22"-23" around crown
- ❑ Sewing thread to match hat
- ❑ Sewing and tapestry needles
- ❑ No. 3 steel hook or hook needed to obtain gauge

Gauge: Rnd 4 = 2" diameter; 4 mesh = 1"; 1 block = 3/8"; 10 dc rows = 3".

Basic Stitches: Ch, sl st, sc, dc.

Special Stitches: For **mesh,** dc in next st, ch 2, skip next 2 chs or sts.

For **beginning mesh (beg mesh),** ch 5, skip next 2 chs or sts.

For **block,** dc in next st, 2 dc in next ch sp.

For **beginning block (beg block),** ch 3, 2 dc in next ch sp.

For **mesh increase (inc),** dc in next st, ch 2, dc in next ch sp, ch 2.

For **mesh decrease (dec),** (skip next st, dc in next ch sp, ch 2) 2 times, skip next st and ch sp.

Crown

Rnd 1: Ch 6, sl st in first ch to form ring, ch 3, 11 dc in ring, join with sl st in top of ch-3. *(12 dc made)*

Rnd 2: Ch 4, (dc, ch 1) in each st around, join with sl st in third ch of ch-4. *(12 dc, 12 ch-1 sps)*

Rnd 3: Ch 4, dc in next ch sp, ch 1, (dc in next st, ch 1, dc in next ch sp, ch 1) around, join. *(24 dc, 24 ch-1 sps)*

Rnd 4: Ch 4, skip next ch sp, (dc in next st, ch 1, skip next ch sp) around, join.

Rnd 5: Ch 4, dc in next ch sp, ch 1, (dc in next st, ch 1, dc in next ch sp, ch 1) around, join. *(48 dc, 48 ch-1 sps)*

Rnd 6: Ch 5, skip next ch sp, (dc in next st, ch 2, skip next ch sp) around, join with sl st in third ch of ch-5. *(48 dc, 48 ch-2 sps)*

Rnd 7: Beg mesh *(see Special Stitches),* **mesh** around, join. *(48 mesh)*

Rnd 8: Beg block *(see Special Stitches),* mesh 3 times, (**block,** mesh 3 times) around, join with sl st in top of ch-3. *(36 mesh, 12 blocks)*

Rnd 9: Beg mesh, block, (mesh, block) around, join. *(24 mesh, 24 blocks)*

Rnd 10: Beg block, mesh, **inc** *(see Special Stitches),* mesh, (block, mesh, inc, mesh) around, join. *(48 mesh, 12 blocks)*

Rnds 11–12: Beg mesh, mesh around, join. *(60 mesh)*

Rnd 13: Beg block, mesh, inc 2 times, mesh, (block, mesh, inc 2 times, mesh) around, join. *(72 mesh, 12 blocks)*

Rnd 14: Beg mesh, block, mesh 4 times, block, (mesh, block, mesh 4 times, block) around, join. *(60 mesh, 24 blocks)*

Rnd 15: Beg block, mesh 6 times, (block, mesh 6 times) around, join. *(72 mesh, 12 blocks)*

Rnd 16: Beg mesh, mesh around, join. *(84 mesh)*

Rnd 17: Beg mesh, mesh 2 times, **dec** *(see Special Stitches),* (mesh 4 times, dec) 11 times, mesh, join. *(72 mesh)*

Rnd 18: Beg block, mesh 2 times, (block, mesh 2 times) around, join. Fasten off. *(48 mesh, 24 blocks)*

Row 19: For **first point,** working in rows, skip first block on rnd 18, join with sl st in dc of next mesh, beg block, mesh 3 times, block, dc in next st leaving remaining sts unworked, turn. *(2 blocks, 3 mesh, 1 dc)*

Row 20: Sl st in first 4 sts, beg block, mesh, block, dc in next st leaving last 3 sts unworked, turn. *(2 blocks, 1 mesh, 1 dc)*

Row 21: Sl st in next 4 sts, beg block, dc in next st. Fasten off. *(1 block, 1 dc)*

Rows 19–21: For **each remaining point,** skipping next block on rnd 18, repeat rows 19–21 of first point.

Sew Crown over top of hat. Sew points to Brim.

50's Style Slippers

Designed by Marion Kelley

Finished Size: 8" sole.

Materials:
- ❏ Worsted yarn:
    - 3 oz. white (pink for Ballet Slippers)
    - 1½ oz. black (white for Ballet Slippers)
- ❏ Pair of 35" shoelaces
- ❏ Safety pin
- ❏ G hook or hook needed to obtain gauge

Gauge: 4 sc = 1"; 4 sc rows = 1".

Basic Stitches: Ch, sl st, sc, hdc, dc.

Saddle Shoe Slipper (make 2)

Rnd 1: With white, ch 26 loosely, 2 sc in second ch from hook, sc in next 9 chs, hdc in next 4 chs, dc in next 8 chs, 2 dc in next ch, hdc in next ch, 5 sc in last ch; working in remaining lps on opposite side of starting ch, hdc in next ch, 2 dc in next ch, dc in next 8 chs, hdc in next 4 chs, sc in next 9 chs, 2 sc in st ch. **Do not join or turn.** *(57 sts made)*

Rnd 2: 2 sc in next st *(mark center back of Slipper with safety pin),* 2 sc in next st, sc in next 24 sts, (2 sc in next st, sc in next st) 2 times, 2 sc in next st, sc in next 24 sts, 2 sc in each of last 2 sts. *(64)*

Rnd 3: Sc in next st, 2 sc in next st, sc in next 25 sts, (2 sc in next st, sc in each of next 2 sts) 3 times, 2 sc in next st, sc in next 25 sts, 2 sc in next st, sc in last st. *(70)*

Rnd 4: Sc in next st, 2 sc in next st, sc in next 28 sts, (2 sc in next st, sc in each of next 2 sts) 3 times, 2 sc in next st, sc in next 28 sts, 2 sc in next st, sc in last st. *(76)*

Rnds 5–8: Keeping safety pin at center back of Slipper, sc in each st around.

Rnd 9: Sc in next 25 sts, (hdc next 2 sts tog, hdc in next 10 sts) 2 times, hdc next 2 sts tog, sc in last 25 sts. *(73)*

Rnd 10: Sc in next 25 sts, (hdc next 2 sts tog, hdc in next 9 sts) 2 times, hdc next 2 sts tog, sc in last 24 sts. *(70)*

Rnd 11: Sc in next 25 sts, (hdc next 2 sts tog, hdc in next 8 sts) 2 times, hdc next 2 sts tog, sc in last 23 sts. *(67)*

Rnd 12: Sc in next 22 sts, hdc next 2 sts tog, hdc in each of next 3 sts, (hdc next 2 sts tog, hdc in next 4 sts) 2 times, hdc next 2 sts tog, hdc in each of next 3 sts, hdc next 2 sts tog, sc in last 21 sts. *(62)*

Rnd 13: Sc in next 20 sts, (hdc next 2 sts tog, hdc in each of next 3 sts) 4 times, hdc next 2 sts tog, sc in last 20 sts. *(57)*

Rnd 14: (Sc in each of next 3 sts, sc next 2 sts tog) 11 times, sc in each of last 2 sts. *(46)*

Rnd 15: (Sc in each of next 3 sts, sc next 2 sts tog) 9 times, sc in last st, join with sl st in first sc. Fasten off.

Strap

Row 1: With black and right side of Slipper facing you, working between rnds 5 and 6, work 12 sc positioned so Strap will come up over top of foot, turn. *(12 sc made)*

Rows 2–11: Ch 1, 2 sc in first st, skip next st, (2 sc in next st, skip next st) across *(last st is skipped)*, turn.

Row 12: Ch 1, sc in next st, (ch 1, skip next st, sc in each of next 2 sts) 3 times, ch 1, skip next st, sc in last st, turn.

Row 13: Ch 1, sc in each st and in each ch across. Fasten off.

Work second Strap on other side of Slipper.

Bring Straps together at top of Slipper and lace with shoelace.

Ballet Slippers

Using pink for white and white for black; work same as Saddle Shoe Slippers.

Lace with ribbon. ✿

Hooded Scarf

Designed by Sharon Muir

Finished Size: Lady's one size fits all.

Materials:
- ❏ 11 oz. purple fuzzy sport yarn
- ❏ K hook or hook needed to obtain gauge

Gauge: 2 shells and 1 sc = 3½"; 3 pattern rows = 2".

Basic Stitches: Ch, sl st, sc, dc.

Special Stitch: For **shell,** 5 dc in ch sp or st.

Scarf

Row 1: Ch 274, 2 dc in fourth ch from hook, (*skip next 2 chs, sc in next ch, skip next 2 chs*; **shell**—*see Special Stitch)* 44 times; repeat between first and second*, 3 dc in last ch, turn. *(44 shells made)*

Row 2: Ch 1, sc in first st, (shell in next st, sc in center st of next shell) 45 times, skip next 2 sts, sc in last st, turn.

Row 3: (Ch 3, 2 dc) in first st, (sc in center st of next shell, shell in next sc) 44 times, sc in center st of last shell, 3 dc in last st, turn.

Rows 4–21: Repeat rows 2 and 3 alternately. At end of last row, **do not turn.**

Rnd 22: *Working in ends of rows, (ch 3, 2 dc) in first row, (sc in next row, skip next row, shell in next row, skip next row) 5 times*; working in remaining lps on opposite side of starting ch on row 1, sc in first ch, (skip next 2 chs, shell in next ch, skip next 2 chs, sc in next ch) 45 times; repeat between first * and second, sl st in top of first ch-3 on row 21. Fasten off.

For **hood,** fold Scarf in half crosswise, right sides together, matching sts; working through both thicknesses, join with sc in first st at fold, sc in next 33 sts leaving remaining sts unworked. Fasten off.

Fringe

For each **Fringe** *(see Stitch Guide),* cut five strands each 18" long. With all five strands held together, fold in half, insert hook in sc, pull fold through st, pull ends through fold, tighten.

Fringe in each sc on each short end of Scarf. ⚘

Lace Mitts

Designed by Michelle Linton

Finished Size: One size fits all.

Materials:
- ❑ 150 yds. size 20 crochet cotton thread
- ❑ No. 10 steel hook or hook needed to obtain gauge

Gauge: 7 sc, 6 ch sps = 2"; 3 ch sps rows = ½".

Basic Stitches: Ch, sl st, sc, tr.

Mitt (make 2)

Rnd 1: Ch 90, sl st in first ch to form ring, ch 5, skip next 4 chs, (sc in next ch, ch 5, skip next 4 chs) around, join with sc in first ch sp. *(18 ch sps made)*

Rnds 2–6: (Sc in next ch sp, ch 5) around, join.

Rnd 7: Ch 5, sc in first ch sp, ch 5, (sc in next ch sp, ch 5) around, join. *(19 ch sps)*

Rnd 8: Ch 5, (sc, ch 5, sc) in next ch sp, ch 5, (sc in next ch sp, ch 5) around, join. *(20 ch sps)*

Rnd 9: (Ch 5, sc in next ch sp) 18 times, ch 5, sc in same ch sp as last sc, ch 5, sc in last ch sp, ch 5, join. *(21 ch sps)*

Rnd 10: (Sc in next ch sp, ch 5) around, join.

Rnd 11: (Ch 5, sc in next ch sp) 19 times, ch 5, sc in same ch sp as last sc, ch 5, sc in last ch sp, ch 5, join. *(22 ch sps)*

Rnds 12–15: (Sc in next ch sp, ch 5) around, join.

Rnd 16: (Ch 5, sc in next ch sp) 16 times; for **thumb opening,** ch 8, skip next 4 ch sps; sc in next ch sp, ch 5, join. *(18 ch sps)*

Rnds 17–19: (Sc in next ch sp, ch 5) around, join.

Rnd 20: For **edging,** (sl st, ch 4; for **picot, ch 3, sl st in third ch from hook;** tr) in first ch sp, (picot, tr in same ch sp as last tr) 5 times, skip next ch sp; *for **scallop,** tr in next ch sp, (picot, tr in same ch sp as last tr) 6 times;* skip next ch sp; repeat from * around, join with sl st in top of ch-4.

Rnd 21: Ch 1, sc in first st, (picot 5 times, skip next 5 sts, sc in each of next 2 sts) 8 times, picot 5 times, skip next 5 sts, sc in last st, join with sl st in first sc.

Rnd 22: Ch 1, sc in first st, (picot 5 times, skip next 5 picots, sc in each of next 2 sts) 8 times, picot 5 times, skip next 5 picots, sc in last st, join. Fasten off.

Wrist Edging

Rnd 1: Working in remaining lps on opposite side of starting ch on rnd 1 of Mitt, join with sl st in any ch sp, ch 4, (picot, tr in same ch sp as ch-4) 6 times, scallop in each ch sp around, join with sl st in top of ch-4.

Rnd 2: Ch 1, sc in first st, (picot 5 times, skip next 5 sts, sc in each of next 2 sts) 17 times, picot 5 times, skip next 5 sts, sc in last st, join with sl st in first sc.

Rnd 3: Ch 1, sc in first st, (picot 5 times, skip next 5 picots, sc in each of next 2 sts) 17 times, picot 5 times, skip next 5 picots, sc in last st, join. Fasten off. ✒

Hairdo Twisties

Designed by Juanita Turner

Finished Size: One size fits all.

Basic Stitches: Ch, sl st, sc, hdc, dc, tr.

Notes: When working all stitches over the ponytail holder *(see Stitch Guide),* the stitches should slide smoothly over the holder *(holder is referred to as ring in instructions).*

When **changing colors** *(see Stitch Guide),* work stitches up to last 2 lps on hook, drop color being used to wrong side of work; with new color, yo, pull through both lps on hook.

Twisties No. 1

Materials:
- ❏ Size 5 pearl cotton:
  25 yds. each black, gold and aqua
- ❏ Braided elastic ponytail holder
- ❏ G hook

Twistie
Working over ring *(see Notes),* holding all three colors of thread together as one, join with sc in ring, ch 15, (sc in ring, ch 15) 39 times, join with sl st in first sc. Fasten off.

Twisties No. 2

Materials:
- ❏ 25 yds. purple eyelash novelty yarn
- ❏ 25 yds. purple cotton sport yarn
- ❏ Braided elastic ponytail holder
- ❏ G hook

No. 3

No. 2

Twistie
Rnd 1: Working over ring *(see Notes),* holding eyelash yarn and cotton sport yarn together as one, join with sc in ring, ch 15, (sc in ring, ch 15) 19 times, **do not join.** *(20 ch lps made)*

Rnd 2: Working in ring between sc of rnd 1, sc between first 2 sts, ch 15, (sc between next 2 sts, ch 15) around, join with sl st in first sc of rnd 1. Fasten off.

Twisties No. 3

Materials:
- ❏ 50 yds. metallic gold braided thread
- ❏ 50 yds. metallic black multicolored thread
- ❏ Braided elastic ponytail holder
- ❏ G hook

Twistie
Rnd 1: Working over ring *(see Notes),* holding both metallic threads together as one, join
continued on page 134

No. 10

No. 7

No. 5

No. 8

No. 6

No. 4

No. 1

No. 11

No. 9

No. 12

continued from page 132

with sc in ring, ch 5, (sc in ring, ch 5) 39 times, join with sl st in first sc. *(40 ch lps made)*

Rnd 2: Ch 1, (sc, hdc, dc, tr, ch 3, sl st in top of last tr made, tr, dc, hdc, sc) in each ch-5 lp around, join. Fasten off.

Twisties No. 4

Materials:
- ❏ 60 yds. acrylic sport yarn
- ❏ Eighty 4mm gold beads
- ❏ Braided elastic ponytail holder
- ❏ G hook

Twistie
String all beads onto yarn before starting, pull up bead as needed.

Working over ring *(see Notes),* join with sc in ring, ch 7, pull up bead, ch 7, (sc in ring, ch 7, pull up bead, ch 7) 79 times, join with sl st in first sc. Fasten off. *(80 ch lps made)*

Twisties No. 5

Materials:
- ❏ Plastic canvas yarn:
  10 yds. each red, white and blue
- ❏ Braided elastic ponytail holder
- ❏ G hook

Twistie
Working over ring *(see Notes),* with all three colors held together as one, join with sc in ring; now using one strand at a time; for **triple loops,** with red, ch 15, drop red lp from hook; with white, ch 15, drop white lp from hook; with blue, ch 15, pick up red and white lps on hook, (holding all three colors together as one, sc in ring, work triple loops) 16 times, holding all three colors together as one, join with sl st in first sc. Fasten off.

Twisties No. 6

Materials:
- ❏ Size 5 pearl cotton:
  25 yds. each rose, gold and blue
- ❏ Braided elastic ponytail holder
- ❏ No. 7 steel hook

Twistie
Rnd 1: Working over ring *(see Notes),* join rose with sc in ring, (ch 7, sc in ring) 20 times, changing to gold in last st made *(see Notes);* (ch 7, sc in ring) 20 times, changing to blue in last st made; ch 7, (sc in ring, ch 7) 19 times, join with sl st in first sc, **turn, do not fasten off.** *(20 ch lps each rose, gold and blue)*

Rnd 2: Ch 1, (5 sc, ch 5, sc, ch 7, sc, ch 5, 5 sc) in each blue ch lp, changing to gold in last st made; repeat between ( ) in each gold ch lp, changing to rose in last st made; repeat between ( ) in each rose ch lp, join. Fasten off.

Twisties No. 7

Materials:
- ❏ 85 yds. off-white size 10 crochet cotton thread
- ❏ Braided elastic ponytail holder
- ❏ No. 7 steel hook

Twistie
Rnd 1: Working over ring *(see Notes),* join with sc in ring, ch 8; for **picot, sl st in fifth ch from hook;** ch 3, (sc in ring, ch 8, picot, ch 3) 39 times, join with sl st in first sc. *(40 ch sps made)*

Rnd 2: Sl st in each ch across to first picot, (sl st, ch 3, 4 dc) in first picot, ch 2; for **shell, (2 dc, ch 2, 2 dc)** in next picot, ch 2, (5 dc in next picot, ch 2, shell in next picot, ch 2) around, join with sl st in top of ch-3. *(20 shells, 20 5-dc groups)*

Rnd 3: Ch 4, (dc in next st, ch 1) 3 times, dc in next st, ch 2, shell in ch sp of next shell, ch 2, *(dc in next st, ch 1) 4 times, dc in next st, ch 2, shell in next shell, ch 2; repeat from * around, join with sl st in third ch of beginning ch-4.

Rnd 4: (Sl st, ch 1, sc) in first ch-1 sp, (ch 3, sc in next ch-1 sp) 3 times, ch 2, shell in next shell, ch 2, *sc in next ch-1 sp, (ch 3, sc in next ch-1 sp) 3 times, ch 2, shell in next shell, ch 2; repeat from * around, join with sl st in first sc.

Rnd 5: (Sl st, ch 1, sc) in first ch-3 sp, (ch 3, sc in next ch-3 sp) 2 times, ch 2, (2 dc, ch 2, 2 dc, ch 2, 2 dc, ch 2) in next shell, *sc in next ch-3 sp, (ch 3, sc in next ch-3 sp) 2 times, ch 2, (2 dc, ch 2, 2 dc, ch 2, 2 dc, ch 2) in next shell; repeat from * around, join.

Rnd 6: (Sl st, ch 1, sc) in first ch-3 sp, ch 3, sc in next ch-3 sp, ch 2, skip next ch-2 sp, (shell, ch 2) in next 2 ch-2 sps, skip next ch-2 sp, *sc in next ch-3 sp, ch 3, sc in next ch-3 sp, ch 2, skip next ch-2 sp, (shell, ch 2) in next 2 ch-2 sps, skip next ch-2 sp; repeat from * around, join. Fasten off.

Twisties No. 8

Materials:
- ❏ 35 yds. white plastic canvas yarn

- ❏ Braided elastic ponytail holder
- ❏ G hook

Twistie

Rnd 1: Working over ring *(see Notes),* join with sc in ring, (ch 7, sc in ring) 29 times, ch 4, join with tr in first sc—*counts as first ch lp. (30 ch lps made)*

Rnd 2: Ch 1, sc in first ch lp, ch 7, (sc in next ch lp, ch 7) around, join with sl st in first sc. Fasten off.

Twisties No. 9

Materials:
- ❏ Size 5 pearl cotton:
    - 50 yds. each pink, burgundy and lime green
- ❏ Braided elastic ponytail holder
- ❏ B hook

Twistie

1: Crochet each color of thread into a long chain, using the entire amount.

2: Holding all three chains together as one, fold in half to find center, tie center to ponytail holder using overhand knot *(see illustration,* keeping knots loose enough to allow holder to slip smoothly through the knot; working down first half of chains, (tie knot in chains 1" down from previous knot; tie chains to ring 1" down from previous knot) across to end of first half.

3: Working with second half of chains, tie knot 1" down from first knot made in step 2; (tie chains to ring 1" down from previous knot, tie knot in chains 1" down from precious knot) across to end of second half. Tie ends of chains together to secure.

Twisties No. 10

Materials:
- ❏ 45 yds. size 10 black/silver metallic thread
- ❏ Braided elastic ponytail holder
- ❏ No. 7 steel hook

Twistie

Rnd 1: Working over ring *(see Notes),* join with

sc in ring, (ch 7, sc in ring) 39 times, ch 4, join with tr in first sc—*counts as first ch lp. (40 ch lps made)*

Rnds 2–3: Ch 1, sc in first ch lp, (ch 7, sc) in each ch lp around, ch 4, join with tr in first sc.

Rnd 4: Ch 7, (sc in next ch lp, ch 7) around, join with sl st in first sc.

Rnd 5: (Sl st, ch 1, sc) in first ch lp, (ch 3, sc) 5 times in same ch lp, ch 3, *sc in next ch lp, (ch 3, sc) 5 times in same ch lp, ch 3; repeat from * around, join. Fasten off.

Twisties No. 11

Materials:
- ❏ Size 10 crochet cotton:
    - 25 yds. each white and pink
- ❏ Braided elastic ponytail holder
- ❏ No. 7 steel hook

Note: Work over each color and pick up when needed.

Twistie

Rnd 1: Working over ring *(see Notes),* join white with sc in ring, ch 9, (sc in ring, ch 9) 39 times, join with sl st in first sc. *(40 ch lps made)*

Rnd 2: Ch 1, 5 sc in first ch lp changing to pink in last st made *(see Stitch Guide),* (sc, ch 7, sc) 5 times in same ch lp, sl st in top of first pink sc made, changing to white, 5 sc in same ch lp; *5 sc in next ch lp, changing to pink, (sc, ch 7, sc) 5 times in same ch lp, sl st in top of first pink sc made in this ch lp, changing to white, 5 sc in same ch lp; repeat from * around, join with sl st in top of first sc. Fasten off.

Twisties No. 12

Materials:
- ❏ 20 yds. each multicolored eyelash novelty yarn and cotton sport yarn
- ❏ Braided elastic ponytail holder
- ❏ G hook

Note: Hold eyelash yarn and cotton sport yarn together as one throughout.

Twistie

Working over ring *(see Notes),* join with sc in ring, ch 7, (sc in ring, ch 7) 19 times, join with sl st in first sc. Fasten off. *(20 ch lps made)* ❦

Dream Catcher Jewelry

Designed by Clare Stringer

Finished Sizes: Earrings are 2½" to 3¾" long; Necklace Pendant is 2½" long.

Materials:
- ❑ Sewing thread:
    Turquoise
    White
    Gold metallic
- ❑ Small amount white size 30 crochet cotton thread
- ❑ Small amount gold filament
- ❑ 1 brown 4mm round bead
- ❑ 2 turquoise 4mm round beads
- ❑ 4 gold 4mm round beads
- ❑ 4 each red, dk. blue, lt. blue, and green seed beads
- ❑ 10 brown seed beads
- ❑ 34 clear seed beads
- ❑ Package small bird feathers
- ❑ One 1¾"-diameter hoop *(for necklace)*
- ❑ One ⅞"-diameter silver jump ring *(for necklace)*
- ❑ Desired size necklace
- ❑ Two 1"-diameter rings
- ❑ Two 1¼"-diameter rings
- ❑ Three ¼" silver bails
- ❑ Pair of ⅞"-diameter hoop post earrings
- ❑ Pair of 1"-long French wire earrings
- ❑ Craft glue
- ❑ Beading and sewing needles
- ❑ No. 8 steel hook

Basic Stitches: Ch, sl st, sc, hdc, dc, tr.

Turquoise Set
Earring (make 2)
Rnd 1: With two strands of turquoise sewing thread held together as one, ch 6, sl st in first ch to form ring, ch 5, (dc in ring, ch 2) 6 times, join with sl st in third ch of ch-5. *(7 ch sps made)*

Rnd 2: (Sl st, ch 1, sc) in first ch sp, (ch 4, sc in next ch sp) 6 times, ch 1, join with dc in first sc *(joining ch sp made).*

Rnd 3: Ch 1, sc in joining ch sp, (ch 6, sc in next ch sp) 6 times, ch 3, join with dc in first sc.

Rnd 4: Ch 1; holding 1"-diameter ring above last rnd, work 15 sc around ring *(see Stitch Guide),* ch 1, (sl st in next ch sp on last rnd, ch 1, work 15 sc around ring, ch 1) around, join with sl st in first sc. Fasten off.

Position top of sc sts on rnd 4 along outer edge on ring, stretching last rnd of crochet piece slightly.

With turquoise thread and beading needle, sew one brown seed bead to any sc on rnd 2.

Tack or glue two small brown feathers to rnd 4 on one side of ring.

Open end on one bail, center one end over last rnd on crochet ring and other end over hoop on earring post, close openings.

Necklace Pendant
Rnds 1–3: Work rnds 1–3 of Earring.

Rnd 4: Ch 1, sc in joining ch sp, (ch 8, sc in next ch sp) 6 times, ch 5, join with tr in first sc *(joining ch sp made).*

Rnd 5: Ch 1, holding 1¾"-diameter ring above last rnd, work 10 sc around ring, ch 1, sl st in next sc on last rnd, ch 1, work 10 sc around ring, ch 1, (sl st in next ch sp on last rnd, ch 1, work 10 sc around ring, ch 1, sl st in next sc on last rnd, ch 1, work 10 sc around ring, ch 1) around, join with sl st in first sc. Fasten off.

Position top of sc sts on rnd 5 along outer edge on ring, stretching last rnd of crochet piece slightly.

With turquoise thread and beading needle, sew one brown 4mm bead to any sc on rnd 2.

Tack or glue three feathers to one side of hoop.

Open ends on one bail, center one end over last rnd on crochet ring and other end over ⅞"-diameter jump ring, close openings. Place Necklace Pendant over chain on necklace.

Gold & White Earrings
Earring (make 2)
Rnd 1: Holding one strand white crochet thread and one strand gold metallic sewing thread together as one, ch 7, dc in seventh ch from hook, ch 3, (dc in same ch, ch 3) 3 times, join with sl st in third ch of ch-7. *(5 dc made)*

Rnd 2: Ch 7, hdc in next dc, (ch 5, hdc in next dc) around, ch 2, join with dc in second ch of ch-7 *(joining ch sp made). (5 ch sps)*

Rnd 3: Ch 1, sc in joining ch sp, ch 3, sc in next hdc, (ch 3, sc in next ch sp, ch 3, sc in next hdc) around, ch 3, join with sl st in first sc.

Rnd 4: Ch 1, holding 1¼"-diameter ring above last rnd, work 8 sc around ring, (sl st in next sc on last rnd, work 8 sc around ring) around, join with sl st in first sc. Fasten off.

For **first tassel,** thread beading needle with filament, tack to bottom of rnd 4 on crochet ring, continued on page 140

Hat & Scarf Set

Designed by Suzann Thompson

Finished Sizes: Scarf is 82" long. Small Hat fits 18" head; large Hat fits 20" head.

Materials:
- ❑ Worsted yarn:
    - 9½ oz. variegated
    - 7½ oz. red
    - 4 oz. yellow
- ❑ 5"-square piece of cardboard
- ❑ Tapestry needle
- ❑ I hook or hook needed to obtain gauge

Gauge: 6 sts = 2"; 4 sc rows and 3 dc rows = 2½".

Basic Stitches: Ch, sl st, sc, dc.

Special Stitch: For **cluster front post (cl fp)**, yo, insert hook around post of sc *(post st, see Stitch Guide)* 2 rows below, yo, pull up long lp, yo, pull through 2 lps on hook, (yo, insert hook around same sc, yo, pull long lp up, yo, pull through 2 lps on hook) 2 times, yo, pull through all 4 lps on hook.

Notes: When **changing colors** *(see Stitch Guide),* drop first color to wrong side of work, pick up when needed. Always change colors in last st made.

Scarf

Row 1: With red, ch 248 loosely, sc in second ch from hook, sc in each ch across, turn. *(Front of row 1 is right side of work—247 sc made)*

Row 2: Ch 3, dc in each st across changing to variegated in last st made *(see Note),* turn.

Row 3: Ch 1, sc in first 3 sts, **cl fp** *(see Special Stitch),* (sc in next 7 sts, cl fp) 30 times, sc in last 3 sts, turn.

Row 4: Ch 3, dc in each st across changing to yellow in last st, turn.

Row 5: Ch 1, sc in each st across, turn.

Row 6: Ch 3, dc in each st across changing to variegated in last st, turn.

Row 7: Ch 1, sc in first 7 sts, (cl fp, sc in next 7 sts) across, turn.

Row 8: Ch 3, dc in each st across changing to red in last st, turn.

Row 9: Ch 1, sc in each st across, turn.

Row 10: Ch 3, dc in each st across changing to variegated, turn.

Rows 11-18: Repeat rows 3–10.

Row 19: Ch 1, sc in first 3 sts, cl fp, (sc in next 7 sts, cl fp) 30 times, sc in last 3 sts. Fasten off.

For each **Fringe** *(see Stitch Guide),* cut five strands each 12" long using same color as row. Hold strands together and fold in half, insert hook in end of row, pull fold through row, pull ends through fold, tighten.

Matching colors, Fringe in ends of dc rows.

continued on page 140

Hat & Scarf Set

continued from page 139

Hat

Note: Instructions are for small; changes for large are in [ ].

Rnd 1 [1]: With yellow [red], ch 3, sl st in first ch to form ring, ch 3, 9 dc in ring, join with sl st in top of ch-3. *(10 dc made)*

Rnd 2 [2]: Ch 1, 2 sc in each st around, join with sl st in first sc. *(20 sc)*

Rnd 3 [3]: (Ch 3, dc) in first st, dc in next st, (2 dc in next st, dc in next st) around, join. *(30 dc)*

Rnd 4 [4]: Ch 1, sc in first 2 sts, 2 sc in next st, (sc in next 2 sts, 2 sc in next st) around, join. *(40 sc)*

Rnd 5 [5]: (Ch 3, dc) in first st, dc in next 3 sts, (2 dc in next st, dc in next 3 sts) around, join. *(50 dc)*

Rnd 6 [6]: Ch 1, sc in each st around, join with sl st in first sc.

Rnd 7: For **small only,** ch 3, dc in each st around, join.

Rnd [7]: For **large only,** (ch 3, dc) in first st, dc in next 4 sts, (2 dc in next st, dc in next 4 sts) around, join. *(60 dc)*

Rnd 8 [8]: Ch 1, sc in each st around, join.

Rnd 9 [9]: Ch 3, dc in each st around, join.

Rnds 10-19 [10-21]: Repeat rnds 8 and 9 alternately. At end of last rnd, **turn.**

Rnd 20: For **small size only;** for **Cuff,** working this rnd only in **back lps** *(see Stitch Guide),* ch 1, sc in first 6 sts, (2 sc in next st, sc in next 7 sts) 2 times, 2 sc in next st, sc in next 8 sts, (2 sc in next st, sc in next 7 sts) 2 times, 2 sc in next st, sc in last 2 sts, join. *(56 sc)*

Rnd [22]: For **large size only;** for **Cuff,** working this rnd only in **back lps** *(see Stitch Guide),* ch 1, sc in first 7 sts, (2 sc in next st, sc in next 14 sts) 3 times, 2 sc in next st, sc in last 7 sts, join. *(64 sc)*

Rnd 21 [23]: Ch 3, dc in each st around, join. Fasten off.

Rnd 22 [24]: Join variegated with sc in first st, sc in next 4 sts, cl fp, (sc in next 7 sts, cl fp) around ending with sc in last 2 sts, join.

Rnd 23 [25]: Ch 3, dc in each st around, join with sl st in top of ch 3. Fasten off.

Rnd 24 [26]: Join red [yellow] with sc in first st, sc in each st around, join.

Rnd 25 [27]: Ch 3, dc in each st around, join. Fasten off.

Rnd 26 [28]: Join variegated with sc in first st, cl fp, (sc in next 7 sts, cl fp) around ending with sc in last 6 sts, join.

Rnd 27 [29]: Ch 3, dc in each st around, join with sl st in top of ch-3. Fasten off.

Rnd 28 [30]: Join yellow [red] with sc in first st, sc in each st around, join.

Rnd 29 [31]: Ch 3, dc in each st around, join. Fasten off.

Rnd 30 [32]: Join variegated with sc in first st, sc in next 4 sts, cl fp, (sc in next 7 sts, cl fp) around ending with sc in last 2 sts, join. Fasten off. Turn Hat right side out; turn Cuff up.

Tassel (optional)

Holding variegated, yellow and red yarn together, wrap around 5"-square cardboard 20 times. Slide off cardboard, cut at one end. Holding all strands together, tie a separate 10" strand of yellow yarn around center of all strands. Fold strands in half at center tie *(see page 43).* Leaving center tie strands loose, wrap separate 10" strand of red yarn several times around all strands 1" from fold, tie ends securely, leaving enough ends to hide inside of Tassel. Using center tie strand at fold, sew to top of Hat. ❧

Dream Catcher Jewelry

continued from page 136

insert threaded beading needle through beads in the following sequence: two clear, one each of dk. green, clear, red, clear, lt. blue, clear, brown, clear, brown, dk. blue, clear, dk. green, clear, brown and clear seed beads, one gold 4mm bead and through one clear seed bead, going back up through all beads, tack to bottom of rnd 4 on crochet ring at same place to secure tassel.

For **second tassel,** thread beading needle with filament, tack to bottom of rnd 4 on crochet ring beside first tassel, insert threaded beading needle through beads in the following sequence: one 4mm turquoise, two clear seed beads, one each of brown, clear, dk. blue, clear, lt. blue, clear, red, clear, dk. green seed beads and one gold 4mm bead, one clear seed bead, going back up through all beads and tack to bottom of rnd 4 on crochet ring in same place.

Tack or glue two small brown feathers to rnd 4 on one side of hoop.

Open loop end on French wire earring and center over last rnd on crochet ring, close opening. ❧

Easy Afghans

Chapter Eight — Warm Up to These Weekend Wonders!

When it's icy outside, nothing is quite as nice as a roaring fire, a cup of tea and a winter warmer! And nothing can warm the heart (not to mention the toes!) like these quick-as-a-wink-to-make afghan designs!

Circles in Squares

Designed by Emily Armstrong

Finished Size: 50" × 80".

Materials:
- ❑ Worsted yarn:
  - 43 oz. white
  - 19 oz. rose
- ❑ Tapestry needle
- ❑ I hook or hook needed to obtain gauge

Gauge: 3 dc = 1"; 3 dc rows = 2".

Basic Stitches: Ch, sl st, sc, dc.

Motif (make 40 white, 28 rose)
Rnd 1: Ch 8, sl st in first ch to form ring, ch 3, 15 dc in ring, join with sl st in top of ch-3. *(16 dc made)*

Rnd 2: Ch 5, (dc in next st, ch 2) 15 times, join with sl st in third ch of ch-5. *(16 dc, 16 ch sps)*

Rnd 3: (Sl st, ch 3, 2 dc) in first ch sp, ch 1, (3 dc in next ch sp, ch 1) 15 times, join with sl st in top of ch-3. *(48)*

Rnd 4: Sl st in each of next 2 sts, ch 1, *sc in next ch sp, (ch 3, sc in next ch sp) 3 times, ch 6; repeat from * 3 more times, join with sl st in first sc.

Rnd 5: (Sl st, ch 3, 2 dc) in first ch sp, 3 dc in each of next 2 ch sps; *for **corner, (5 dc, ch 2, 5 dc) in next ch-6 sp;** 3 dc in each of next 3 ch sps; repeat from * 2 more times, corner, join with sl st in top of ch-3.

Rnd 6: Ch 3, dc in each st around with (dc, tr, dc) in each corner ch sp, join. Fasten off.

Finishing
With white, alternating eight white rows and seven red rows, sew Motifs together according to diagram below.

Edging
Join white with sc in any st, sc in each st and in each seam around with 3 sc in each tr, join with sl st in first sc. Fasten off.

Tassel (make 22)
Cut 18 strands white each 18" long; tie separate 5" strand around center of all strands held together leaving ends for tying *(see page 43)*. Fold strands in half, tie separate strand around all strands 1" from fold.

Tie one Tassel to sc at each point and each seam between points on each short end of Afghan. ❀

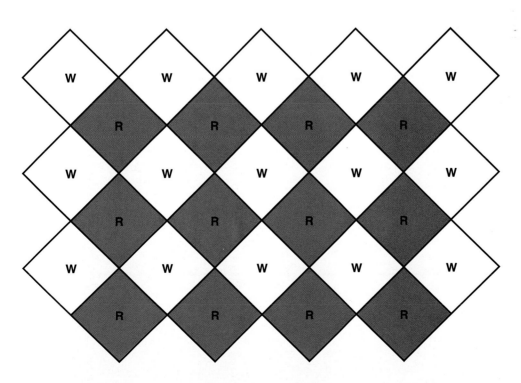

Textured Stripes

Designed by Dorris Brooks

Finished Size: 43" × 68½".

Materials:
- ❑ Worsted yarn:
  - 26 oz. burgundy
  - 14 oz. each pink and rose
- ❑ H hook or hook needed to obtain gauge

Gauge: 2 double cross sts and 2 dc = 2¾"; 4 double cross st rows = 3".

Basic Stitches: Ch, sl st, dc, tr.

Afghan

Row 1: With burgundy, ch 156, sc in second ch from hook, sc in each ch across, turn. *(155 sc made)*

Row 2: Ch 3, dc in each of next 2 sts; for **double cross st (dbl cross st), skip next 2 sts, tr in next 2 sts, working behind last 2 tr worked, tr in first skipped st, tr in next skipped st;** (dc in next st, dbl cross st) 29 times, dc in each of last 3 sts, turn. *(30 dbl cross sts, 35 dc)*

Row 3: Ch 3, dc in next st, **tr fp** *(see Stitch Guide)* around next st, (dbl cross st, tr fp around next st) across to last 2 sts, dc in each of last 2 sts, turn.

Row 4: Ch 3, dc in next st, tr bp around next st, (dbl cross st, tr bp around next st) across to each of last 2 sts, dc in each of last 2 sts, turn.

Rows 5–6: Repeat rows 3 and 4. At end of last row, fasten off.

Row 7: Join rose with sl st in first st, ch 3, dc in next st, tr fp around next st, (dbl cross st, tr fp around next st) across to last 2 sts, dc in each of last 2 sts, turn.

Rows 8–9: Repeat rows 4 and 3. At end of last row, fasten off.

Row 10: Join pink with sl st in first st, ch 3, dc in next st, tr bp around next st, (dbl cross st, tr bp around next st) across to last 2 sts, dc in each of last 2 sts, turn.

Rows 11–12: Repeat rows 3 and 4. At end of last row, fasten off.

Row 13: Join burgundy with sl st in first st, ch 3, dc in next st, tr fp around next st, (dbl cross st, tr fp around next st) across to last 2 sts, dc in each of last 2 sts, turn.

Rows 14–17: Repeat rows 4 and 3 alternately. At end of last row, fasten off.

Row 18: Join rose with sl st in first st, ch 3, dc in next st, tr bp around next st, (dbl cross st, tr bp around next st) across to last 2 sts, dc in each of last 2 sts, turn.

Rows 19–20: Repeat rows 3 and 4. At end of last row, fasten off.

Row 21: Join pink with sl st in first st, ch 3, dc in next st, tr fp around next st, (dbl cross st, tr fp around next st) across to last 2 sts, dc in each of last 2 sts, turn.

Rows 22–23: Repeat rows 4 and 3. At end of last row, fasten off.

Row 24: Join burgundy with sl st in first st, ch 3, dc in next st, tr bp around next st, (dbl cross st, tr bp around next st) across to last 2 sts, dc in each of last 2 sts, turn.

Rows 25–28: Repeat rows 3 and 4 alternately. At end of last row, fasten off.

Rows 29–94: Repeat rows 7–28 consecutively. At end of last row, **do not fasten off.**

Row 95: Ch 1, sc in each st across, turn. Fasten off.

For each **Fringe** *(see Stitch Guide,* cut three strands each 17" long from burgundy. Hold all three strands together and fold in half, insert hook in st, pull fold through st, pull ends through fold, tighten.

Fringe in first st at end and in every second st across row 95 and row 1. ❁

Medieval Strips

Designed by Deborah Levy-Hamburg

Finished Size: 40" × 76".

Materials:
- ❏ Worsted yarn:
  - 25 oz. red
  - 16 oz. winter white
- ❏ H hook or hook needed to obtain gauge

Gauge: Strip = 4½" wide.

Basic Stitches: Ch, sl st, sc, dc.

Special Stitches: For **puff stitch (puff st)**, (yo, pull up lp) 3 times in same st, yo, pull through all 7 lps on hook, ch 1.

For **2-double crochet cluster (2-dc cl)**, yo, insert hook in next st, yo, pull through 2 lp hook, yo, insert hook in same st, yo, pull through 2 lps on hook, yo, pull through all 3 loops on hook.

Strip (make 7)

Center
Row 1: With red, ch 4, sl st in first ch to form ring, ch 3, (3 dc, ch 3, 4 dc) in ring, turn. *(8 dc, 1 ch sp made)*

Rows 2-100: Ch 3, (3 dc, ch 3, 3 dc) in ch-3 sp, skip 2 dc, dc in last dc, turn. *(8 dc, 1 ch sp)*

Row 101: For top, ch 3, sl st in next 3 chs, ch 3, skip 2 dc, sl st in last dc. Fasten off.

Border
Rnd 1: Join winter white with sl st in bottom ring of Strip Center, ch 1, **(puff st**—*see Special Stitches,* ch 1) 3 times in same ring, puff st in end of row 1, ch 1, (puff st in end of next row, ch 1) 99 times; working across top of Center, puff st in next ch-3 sp, ch 1, covering sl sts,, (puff st, ch 1) 3 times in next ch-3 sp, puff st in next ch-3 sp, ch 1, (puff st in end of next row, ch 1) 99 times, puff st in end of row 1, ch 1, join with sl st in top of first puff st. Fasten off. *(208 puff sts made)*

Rnd 2: Join red with sl st in ch-1 sp before 3 puff sts at one end of Strip, ch 1, (puff st, ch 1) 2 times in same sp, *(puff st, ch 1, puff st, ch 1) in each of next 3 ch-1 sps, (puff st, ch 1) in each of next 100 ch-1 sps, (puff st, ch 1, puff st, ch 1) in each of next 4 ch-1 sps, (puff st, ch 1) in each of next 99 ch-1 sps, join with sl st in first puff st. Fasten off.

Rnd 3: Join winter white with sl st in first ch-1 sp, ch 2, (dc, ch 1, **2-dc cl**—*see Special Stitches,* ch 1) in same sp, (2-dc cl, ch 1, 2-dc cl, ch 1) in each of next 6 ch-1 sps, *covering ch sps as you work, (2-dc cl, ch 1, 2-dc cl, ch 1) in next 100 puff sts on rnd 1*, (2-dc cl, ch 1, 2-dc cl, ch 1) in next 7 ch-1 sps on last rnd; repeat between first and second * one more time, join with sl st in top of first dc. Fasten off. *(216 pairs of 2-dc cls)*

Rnd 4: Join red with sc in first ch-1 sp, (ch 1, skip next 2-dc cl, sc in **back lp** *(see Stitch Guide)* of next ch, ch 1, skip next 2-dc cl, sc in next ch-1 sp) around, join with sl st in first sc.

Rnd 5: Ch 1, sc in same st, (ch 3, skip next sc, sc in next sc) around, ch 3, join with sl st in first sc. Fasten off. Mark center eight ch-3 sps at on each end.

Joining Strips

Join red with sc in first unmarked ch-3 sp at bottom right of Strip #1, ch 3, sc in first unmarked ch-3 sp at bottom left of Strip #2, (ch 3, sc in next ch-3 sp on Strip #1, ch 3, sc in next ch-3 sp on Strip #2) across to marked ch-3 sps at other end of Strips. Fasten off. Repeat to join remaining Strips. ✿

Fluted Flowers

Designed by Maggie Weldon

Finished Size: 46" × 68".

Materials:
- ❑ Worsted yarn:
  - 25 oz. cream
  - 7 oz. peach *(for petals)*
  - 7 oz. rust *(for petals)*
  - 7 oz. teal
- ❑ Tapestry needle
- ❑ I hook or hook needed to obtain gauge

Gauges: Large Motif is 10" across; rnds 1–2 are 3¼" across. Fill-In Motif is 3¼" across.

Basic Stitches: Ch, sl st, sc, dc, tr.

Special Stitches:

For **shell,** (3 dc, ch 3, 3 dc) in next ch sp.

For **joined shell,** 3 dc in next ch-3 sp at corner of this Motif, ch 1, drop lp from hook, insert hook in center ch of corresponding ch-3 sp at corner of previous Motif *(see gray line on assembly illustration below)*, pull dropped lp through ch, ch 2, 3 dc in same ch-3 sp on this Motif.

For **joined ch-5 sp,** sc in next ch-5 sp on this Motif, ch 2, drop lp from hook, insert hook in center of corresponding ch-5 sp of previous Motif *(see red line on assembly illustration)*, pull dropped lp through ch, ch 3, sc in same ch-5 sp on this Motif.

Assembly Illustration

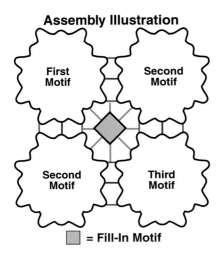

= Fill-In Motif

Motif Center
(make 18 with peach petals, 17 with rust petals)

Rnd 1: With cream, ch 3, sl st in first ch to form ring, ch 4, 15 tr in ring, join with sl st in top of ch-4. *(16 tr made)*

Rnd 2: Ch 1, sc in first st, ch 3, skip next st, (sc in next st, ch 3, skip next st) 7 times, join with sl st in first sc. *(8 sc, 8 ch sps)*

Rnd 3: Ch 1, sc in first st, ch 5, skip next ch sp, (sc in next st, ch 5, skip next ch sp) 7 times, join. Fasten off.

Rnd 4: For **petals,** join petal color with sl st in any ch-3 sp on rnd 2, ch 4, 10 tr in same ch-3 sp as joining sl st, drop lp from hook, insert hook from back to front through top of ch-4, pull dropped lp through st, ch 3, (11 tr in next ch-3 sp, drop lp from hook, insert hook from back to front through top of first tr of group, pull dropped lp through st, ch 3) around, join with sl st in top of ch-4. Fasten off.

Afghan

For **First Row,** work First Motif with peach petals; alternating colors of petals, work Second Motif four times for a total of five Motifs in First Row.

For **Next Row,** alternating colors of petals and joining to last row, work one Second Motif onto first Motif; work Third Motif three times for a total of five Motifs.

Repeat Next Row for a total of seven rows.

Work one Fill-In-Motif in each opening between Motifs.

First Motif

Rnd 1: Working behind petals on rnd 3 of Motif Center, join teal with sl st in any ch-5 sp, ch 3, (dc, ch 2, 2 dc) in same ch sp as last sl st made, (2 dc, ch 2, 2 dc) in each ch-5 sp around, join with sl st in top of ch-3. *(32 dc, 8 ch-2 sps)*

Rnd 2: Ch 3, dc in next st, *(2 dc, ch 2, 2 dc) in next ch-2 sp, dc in each of next 2 sts, sc in next sp between sts, dc in each of next 2 sts; repeat from * 6 more times, (2 dc, ch 2, 2 dc) in next ch-2 sp, dc in each of next 2 sts, sc in last sp between sts, join. Fasten off. *(72 sts, 8 ch-2 sps)*

Rnd 3: Join cream with sc in any ch-2 sp, ch 5, sc in same ch-2 sp as joining sc, ch 3, (dc, ch 3, dc) in next sc, ch 3, *(sc, ch 5, sc) in next ch-2 sp, ch 3, (dc, ch 3, dc) in next sc, ch 3; repeat from * around, join with sl st in first sc. *(32 ch sps)*

Rnd 4: Ch 1, (sc, ch 5, sc) in first ch-5 sp, ch 3, skip next ch-3 sp, (2 dc, ch 3, 2 dc) in next ch-3 sp *(corner made)*, ch 3, skip next ch-3 sp, *(sc, ch 5, sc) in next ch-5 sp, ch 3, skip next ch-3 sp, (2 dc, ch 3, 2 dc) in next ch-3 sp *(corner made)*, ch 3, skip next ch-3 sp; repeat from * around, join.

continued on page 151

Wedding Bells

Designed by Deborah Levy-Hamburg

Finished Size: 39" × 58" without Fringe.

Materials:
- ❏ 35 oz. off-white worsted yarn
- ❏ H hook or hook needed to obtain gauge

Gauge: 2 pattern repeats = 6½"; 5 rows = 3".

Basic Stitches: Ch, sl st, dc.

Afghan
Row 1: Ch 139, dc in fourth ch from hook, dc in each of next 3 chs, *skip next 2 chs, 5 dc in next ch *(shell made),* ch 2, skip next 3 chs, dc in next 5 chs; repeat from * across, turn.

Rows 2–96: Ch 3, dc in next 4 sts, *skip next 2 chs, 5 dc in next st, ch 2, skip next 4 sts, dc in next 5 sts; repeat from * across, turn. At end of last row, fasten off.

Fringe
For each **Fringe** *(see Stitch Guide),* cut 16 strands each 12" long. With all strands held together, fold in half, insert hook in st, pull fold through st, pull ends through fold, tighten.

Fringe in each corner and evenly space 23 more across first and last rows of Afghan. ❀

Fluted Flowers

continued from page 149

Rnd 5: Ch 1, (sc, ch 5, sc) in first ch-5 sp, ch 3, skip next ch-3 sp, **shell** *(see Special Stitches)* in ch-3 sp at next corner, ch 3, skip next ch-3 sp, *(sc, ch 5, sc) in next ch-5 sp, ch 3, skip next ch-3 sp, shell in ch-3 sp at next corner, ch 3, skip next ch-3 sp; repeat from * around, join. Fasten off.

Second Motif *(joined on one side)*
Rnds 1–4: Repeat rnds 1–4 of First Motif.

Rnd 5: Ch 1, (sc, ch 5, sc) in first ch-5 sp, ch 3, skip next ch-3 sp, work **joined shell** *(see Special Stitches),* ch 3, skip next ch-3 sp on this Motif, work **joined ch-5 sp** *(see Special Stitches),* ch 3, skip next ch-3 sp on this Motif, work joined shell, ch 3, skip next ch-3 sp on this Motif, *(sc, ch 5, sc) in next ch-5 sp, ch 3, skip next ch-3 sp, shell in ch-3 sp at next corner, ch 3, skip next ch-3 sp; repeat from * around, join. Fasten off.

Third Motif *(joined on two sides)*
Rnds 1–4: Repeat rnds 1–4 of First Motif.

Rnd 5: Ch 1, (sc, ch 5, sc) in first ch-5 sp, ch 3, skip next ch-3 sp, *work joined shell, ch 3, skip next ch-3 sp on this Motif, work joined ch-5 sp, ch 3, skip next ch-3 sp on this Motif, work joined shell, ch 3, skip next ch-3 sp on this Motif, (sc, ch 5, sc) in next ch-5 sp, ch 3, skip next ch-3 sp; repeat from * one more time, shell in ch-3 sp at next corner, ch 3, skip next ch-3 sp, ◊(sc, ch 5, sc) in next ch-5 sp, ch 3, skip next ch-3 sp, shell in ch-3 sp at next corner, ch 3,

skip next ch-3 sp; repeat from ◊ around, join. Fasten off.

Fill-In-Motif
Rnd 1: With cream, ch 3, sl st in first ch to form ring, ch 3, 2 dc in ring, ch 2, (3 dc, ch 2) 3 times in ring, join with sl st in top of ch-3. *(4 ch sps made)*

Rnd 2: Sl st in each of next 2 sts, (sl st, ch 3, 2 dc, ch 2, 3 dc) in next ch-2 sp, ch 1, *(3 dc, ch 2, 3 dc) in next ch-2 sp, ch 1; repeat from * around, join. *(8 ch sps)*

Rnd 3: Working in open edge between Motifs, sl st in each of next 2 sts, (sl st, ch 3, 2 dc) in next ch-2 sp, *◊ch 1, sl st in corresponding worked joining at corner of Motifs *(see blue line on assembly illustration on page 149),* ch 1, 3 dc in same ch-2 sp as last dc made on this Motif, ch 1, sc in next ch-1 sp, drop lp from hook, insert hook in center ch of corresponding ch-5 sp, pull dropped lp through ch, ch 1◊, 3 dc in next ch-2 sp at corner of this Motif; repeat from * 2 more times; repeat between first and second ◊, join. Fasten off.

Edging
With right side of Afghan facing you, join cream with sl st in center ch-5 sp on edge of right-hand corner Motif, (ch 3, dc, ch 3, 3 dc) in same ch-5 sp, work (ch 2, sc, ch 2) in next ch sp, *work shell in next ch sp or joining seam, work (ch 2, sc, ch 2) in next ch sp; repeat from * around, join with sl st in top of first ch-3. Fasten off. ❀

Shamrock

Designed by Paula Pelkey

Finished Size: 58" × 73½".

Materials:
- ❏ 76½ oz. green worsted yarn
- ❏ N hook or hook needed to obtain gauge

Gauge: 2 dc = 1"; 2 dc rows = 2".

Basic Stitches: Ch, sl st, sc, dc.

Note: Use two strands held together throughout.

Afghan
Row 1: Ch 147, dc in fourth ch from hook, dc in each of next 3 chs, *(ch 1, skip next ch, dc in next ch) 5 times, dc in next 4 chs; repeat from * across, turn. *(95 dc, 50 ch sps made)*

Row 2: Ch 3, dc in next 4 sts, *(ch 1, skip next ch sp, dc in next st) 2 times; for **puff stitch (ps)**, yo, insert hook in next ch sp, yo, pull long lp through ch sp, (yo, insert hook in same ch sp, yo, pull long lp through ch sp) 3 times, yo, pull through all 9 loops on hook, ch 1; dc in next st, (ch 1, skip next ch sp, dc in next st) 2 times, dc in next 4 sts; repeat from * across, turn.

Row 3: Ch 3, dc in next 4 sts, (ch 1, skip next ch sp, dc in next st, ps, dc in next st, ch 1, skip next ps, dc in next st, ps, dc in next st, ch 1, skip next ch sp, dc in next 5 sts) across, turn.

Row 4: Ch 3, dc in next 4 sts, (ch 1, skip next ch sp, dc in next st, ch 1, skip next ps, dc in next st, ps, dc in next st, ch 1, skip next ps, dc in next st, ch 1, skip next ch sp, dc in next 5 sts) across, turn.

Row 5: Ch 3, dc in next 4 sts, *(ch 1, skip next ch sp, dc in next st) 2 times, ch 1, skip next ps, dc in next st, (ch 1, skip next ch sp, dc in next st) 2 times, dc in next 4 sts; repeat from * across, turn.

Rows 6–57: Repeat rows 2–5 consecutively.

Rnd 58: Working around outer edge, ch 1, sc in each st, in each ch sp and 2 sc in end of each row around with 3 sc in each corner, join with sl st in first sc. Fasten off. ✳

Field of Flowers

Designed by Zona Robinson

Finished Size: 60" square.

Materials:
- ❑ Baby yarn:
    - 9½ oz. white
    - 5 oz. each blue, green, lavender and pink
    - 2½ oz. each yellow and peach
- ❑ 1½"-square piece of cardboard
- ❑ Tapestry needle
- ❑ G, H and I hooks or hooks needed to obtain gauges

Gauges: **I hook,** 3 dc = 1"; 3 dc rows = 2". Each flower is 3½" across. Each Motif is 5½"-square.

Basic Stitches: Ch, sl st, sc, hdc, dc.

Motif No. 1 (make 4)
Rnd 1: With G hook and yellow, ch 6, sl st in first ch to form ring, ch 3, 15 dc in ring, join with sl st in top of ch-3. *(16 dc made)*

Rnd 2: Ch 9, dc in same st, skip next st, *(dc, ch 6, dc) in next st, skip next st; repeat from * around, join with sl st in third ch of ch-9.

Rnd 3: Ch 1, 3 sc in next ch sp; for **picot, ch 3, sl st in third ch from hook;** 3 sc in same ch sp, (3 sc, picot, 3 sc) in each ch sp around, join with sl st in first sc. Fasten off.

Rnd 4: With H hook and green, join with sl st in any picot, (ch 6, sl st, ch 3, dc) in same picot, ch 1, *(dc, ch 3, sl st, ch 3, dc) in next picot, ch 1; repeat from * around, join with sl st in third ch of ch-6. Fasten off.

Rnd 5: With I hook and white, join with sl st in any ch-1 sp; for **beginning corner (beg corner), (ch 3, 2 dc, ch 2, 3 dc) in same sp;** ch 2; for **shell, 3 dc in next ch-1 sp, ch 2;** *for **corner, (3 dc, ch 2, 3 dc) in next ch-1 sp;** ch 2, shell; repeat from * around, join with sl st in top of ch-3.

Rnd 6: Sl st in each of next 2 sts, sl st in next ch sp, beg corner, shell in each of next 2 ch sps, (corner, shell in each of next 2 ch sps) around, join. Fasten off.

Motif No. 2 (make 12)
Rnd 1: With I hook and peach, ch 2, 8 sc in second ch from hook, join with sl st in **front lp** *(see Stitch Guide)* of first sc. *(8 sc made)*

Rnd 2: Working this rnd in **front lps,** ch 6, (sl st in next st, ch 6) around, join with sl st in **back lp** of first st on rnd 1.

Rnd 3: Working this rnd in **back lps** of rnd 1, ch 10, (sl st in next st, ch 10) around, join with sl st in first ch of first ch-10. Fasten off.

Rnd 4: With H hook and green, join with sl st in any ch sp, (ch 6, sl st, ch 3, dc) in same sp, ch 1, *(dc, ch 3, sl st, ch 3, dc) in next ch sp, ch 1; repeat from * around, join with sl st in third ch of ch-6. Fasten off.

Rnds 5–6: Repeat rnds 5–6 of Motif No. 1.

Motif No. 3 (make 20)
Rnd 1: With H hook and two strands blue held together, ch 2, 8 sc in second ch from hook, join with sl st in first sc. *(8 sc made)*

Rnd 2: *(For **petal, ch 4, dc in fourth ch from hook, ch 5, dc in fourth ch from hook;** sl st in same st*, sl st in next st) 7 times; repeat between first and second*, join with sl st in first ch of first ch-4. Fasten off.

Rnd 3: With H hook and green, join with sl st in ch sp at center of any petal, (ch 6, sl st, ch 3, dc) in same sp, ch 1, *(dc, ch 3, sl st, ch 3, dc) in ch sp at center of next petal, ch 1; repeat from * around, join with sl st in third ch of ch-6. Fasten off.

Rnds 4–5: Repeat rnds 5–6 of Motif No. 1.

Motif No. 4 (make 28)
Rnd 1: With I hook and lavender, ch 5, sl st in first ch to form ring, ch 5, (dc in ring, ch 2) 7 times, join with sl st in third ch of ch-5. *(8 dc, 8 ch sps made)*

Rnd 2: Ch 1, (2 sc, ch 2, 2 sc) in each ch sp around, join with sl st in first sc. Fasten off.

Rnd 3: Repeat rnd 4 of Motif No. 2.

Rnds 4–5: Repeat rnds 5–6 of Motif No. 1.

Motif No. 5 (make 36)
Rnd 1: With H hook and pink, ch 4, sl st in first ch to form ring, ch 1, (sc in ring, ch 3) 8 times, join with sl st in first sc. *(8 sc, 8 ch sps made)*

Rnd 2: Sl st in first ch sp, ch 3, 3 dc in same sp, drop lp from hook, insert hook in third ch of ch-3, pull dropped lp through ch, ch 1; for **popcorn (pc), 4 dc in same ch sp, drop lp from hook, insert hook in top of first dc of group, pull dropped lp through st;** ch 1; *(for **petal, pc, ch 1, pc) in next ch sp;** ch 1; repeat from * around, join with sl st in top of ch-3. Fasten off. *(8 petals)*

Rnd 3: With H hook and green, join with sl st in ch sp after any petal, (ch 6, sl st, ch 3, dc) in same sp, ch 1, skip next petal, *(dc, ch 3, sl st, ch 3, dc) in next ch sp, ch 1, skip next

continued on page 159

Simply Patriotic

Designed by Martha Brooks Stein

Finished Size: 46" × 62".

Materials:
- ❑ Worsted yarn:
    - 20 oz. blue
    - 16 oz. off-white
    - 12 oz. red
- ❑ Tapestry needle
- ❑ H hook or hook needed to obtain gauge

Gauge: Motif = 4" square.

Basic Stitches: Ch, sl st, sc, hdc, dc.

Motif A (make 96)
Rnd 1: With red, ch 6, sl st in first ch to form ring, ch 3, 2 dc in ring, ch 2, (3 dc in ring, ch 2) 3 times, join with sl st in top of ch-3. Fasten off. *(4 ch sps made)*

Rnd 2: Join off-white with sl st in any ch-2 sp; for **beginning shell (beg shell), (ch 3, 2 dc, ch 2, 3 dc) in same ch sp as sl st,** ch 1; for ***shell, (3 dc, ch 2, 3 dc)** in next ch-2 sp, ch 1; repeat from * around, join. Fasten off. *(8 ch sps)*

Rnd 3: Join blue with sl st in any ch-2 sp, beg shell, ch 1, 3 dc in next ch-1 sp, ch 1, (shell in next ch-2 sp, ch 1, 3 dc in next ch-1 sp, ch 1) 3 times, join. Fasten off.

Motif B (make 69)
Rnd 1: With red, ch 6, sl st in first ch to form ring, ch 3, 2 dc in ring, ch 2, (3 dc in ring, ch 2) 3 times, join with sl st in top of ch-3. Fasten off. *(4 ch sps made)*

Rnd 2: Join blue with sl st in any ch-2 sp, beg shell, ch 1, (shell in next ch-2 sp, ch 1) around, join. Fasten off. *(8 ch sps)*

Rnd 3: Join off-white with sl st in any ch-2 sp, beg shell, ch 1, 3 dc in next ch-1 sp, ch 1, (shell in next ch-2 sp, ch 1, 3 dc in next ch-1 sp, ch 1) 3 times, join. Fasten off.

Assembly
Using matching color yarn, sew Motifs together in **inside lps** *(see Inside Loops*
continued on page 158

Simply Patriotic

continued from page 156

illustration below) according to Simply Patriotic Afghan Assembly Diagram below.

Inside Loops Illustration

Border

Rnd 1: Working around outer edge, join blue with sc in any corner ch-2 sp, ch 2, sc in same ch sp, sc in each st, hdc in each seam and sc in each ch-1 sp around with (sc, ch 2, sc) in each corner ch-2 sp, join with sl st in first sc. Fasten off.

Rnd 2: Join red with sc in any corner ch sp, ch 2, sc in same ch sp, (ch 1, skip next st, sc in next st) across to next corner, ch 1, skip next st, *(sc, ch 2, sc) in next corner ch sp, ch 1, skip next st, (sc in next st, ch 1, skip next st) across to next corner; repeat from * around, join. Fasten off.

Rnd 3: Join off-white with sl st in any corner ch sp, ch 3, (sl st in next ch sp, ch 3) around, join with sl st in first sl st. Fasten off. ❀

Simply Patriotic Afghan Assembly Diagram

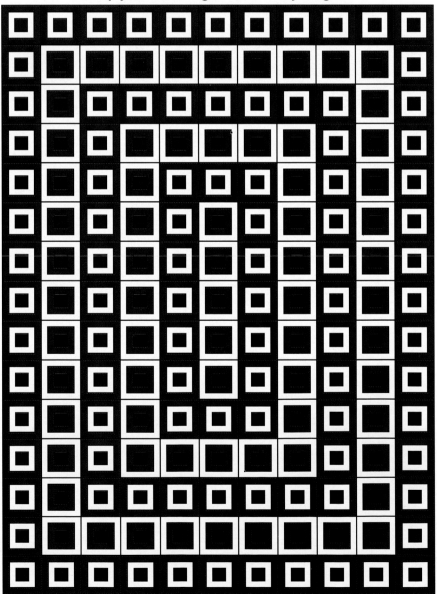

petal; repeat from * around, join with sl st in third ch of ch-6. Fasten off.

Rnds 4–5: Repeat rnds 5–6 of Motif No. 1.

Pom Poms (make 36)

Wrap pink around cardboard 50 times; slide loops off cardboard, tie separate 6" strand pink tightly around center of all loops; cut loops. Trim ends. Sew to center of each pink flower on Motif No. 5. Sew Motifs together through **back lps** according to Field of Flowers Assembly Diagram below.

Edging

Rnd 1: With I hook and white, join with sl st in any corner ch sp, beg corner, ch 1, (3 dc, ch 1) in each ch sp across to next corner, *corner in corner ch sp, ch 1, (3 dc, ch 1) in each ch sp across to next corner; repeat from * 2 more times. *(192 shells, 4 corners made)*

Rnd 2: Ch 3, dc in each st and in each ch around with corner in each corner ch sp, join.

Rnds 3–4: Ch 3, dc in each st around with corner in each corner ch sp, join. At end of last rnd, fasten off.

Rnd 5: Working this rnd in **front lps,** with H hook and yellow, join with sc in any corner ch sp, 2 sc in same ch sp, *[sc in next st, (ch 4, skip next st, sc in next st) across to next corner], 3 sc in next corner ch sp; repeat from * 2 more times; repeat between [ ], join with sl st in first sc. Fasten off.

Rnd 6: With I hook and white, join with sl st in first st of any 3-sc corner group, ch 2, hdc in each of next 2 sts; (*working in **back lps** of rnd 4, hdc in each st across to next corner*, hdc in each of next 3 corner sts) 3 times; repeat between first and second*, join with sl st in top of ch-2. Fasten off. ❀

Field of Flowers Assembly Diagram

5	5	5	5	5	5	5	5	5	5
5	4	4	4	4	4	4	4	4	5
5	4	3	3	3	3	3	3	4	5
5	4	3	2	2	2	2	3	4	5
5	4	3	2	1	1	2	3	4	5
5	4	3	2	1	1	2	3	4	5
5	4	3	2	2	2	2	3	4	5
5	4	3	3	3	3	3	3	4	5
5	4	4	4	4	4	4	4	4	5
5	5	5	5	5	5	5	5	5	5

Stitch Guide

Ounces to Grams	Grams to Ounces
1 = 28.4	25 = 7/8
2 = 56.7	40 = 1 2/5
3 = 85.0	50 = 1 3/4
4 = 113.4	100 = 3 1/2

Chain—ch: Yo, pull through lp on hook.

Single Crochet—sc: Insert hook in st, yo, pull through st, yo, pull through both lps on hook.

Slip stitch—sl st: Insert hook in st, yo, pull through st and lp on hook.

Change Colors: Drop first color; with 2nd color, pull through last 2 lps of st.

Half Double Crochet—hdc: Yo, insert hook in st, yo, pull through st, yo, pull through all 3 lps on hook.

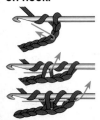

Double Crochet—dc: Yo, insert hook in st, yo, pull through st, (yo, pull through 2 lps) 2 times.

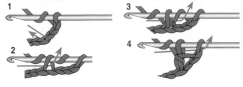

Treble Crochet—tr: Yo 2 times, insert hook in st, yo, pull through st, (yo, pull through 2 lps) 3 times.

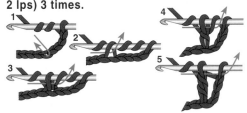

Double Treble Crochet—dtr: Yo 3 times, insert hook in st, yo, pull through st, (yo, pull through 2 lps) 4 times.

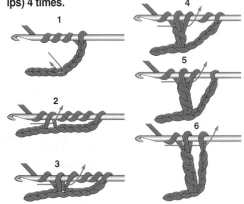

Triple Treble Crochet—ttr: Yo 4 times, insert hook in st, yo, pull through st, (yo, pull through 2 lps) 5 times.

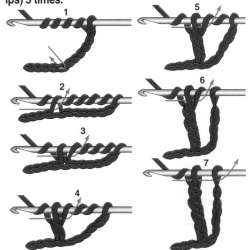

Hook Sizes

U.S.	Metric	U.K.	U.S.	Metric	U.K.
14	0.60mm		6....G	4.50mm	7
12	0.75mm			4.75mm	
10	1.00mm		8...H	5.00mm	6
6	1.50mm		9...I	5.50mm	5
0...5	1.75mm		10..J	6.00mm	4
1...B	2.00mm	14		6.50mm	3
2...C	2.50mm	12	10½K	7.00mm	2
D	3.00mm	10	11	8.00mm	
4...E	3.50mm	9	13	9.00mm	
5...F	4.00mm	8	15..P	10.00mm	
			Q	16.00mm	

Standard Abbreviations

ch, chs .... chain, chains
dc .... double crochet
hdc .... half double crochet
lp, lps .... loop, loops
rnd, rnds .... round, rounds
sc .... single crochet
sl st .... slip stitch
sp, sps .... space, spaces
st, sts .... stitch, stitches
tog .... together
tr .... treble crochet

yo .... yarn over
sc next 2 sts tog—(insert hook in next st, yo, pull through st) 2 times, yo, pull through all 3 lps on hook.
hdc next 2 sts tog—(yo, insert hook in next st, yo, pull through st) 2 times, yo, pull through all 5 lps on hook.
dc next 2 sts tog—(yo, insert hook in next st, yo, pull through st, yo, pull through 2 lps on hook) 2 times, yo, pull through 3 lps on hook.

Embroidery Stitches

Fly Stitch

Straight Stitch

Satin Stitch

French Knot

Backstitch

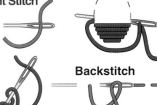
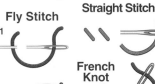

Special Stitches

Reverse Sc

Fringe

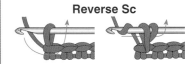

Working around Ring

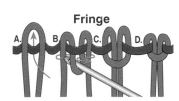

Slip Ring

4" End

Leave ring loose until sts are made.

Front Post Stitch—fp/Back Post Stitch—bp: Yo, insert hook from right to left around post of st on previous row, complete as dc.

Front   Back

Front loop—front lp: Back loop—back lp:

Front Loop   Back Loop

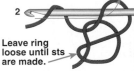